PRAISE FOR *SIMPLY WEALTHY*

"We all participate in the financial industry, whether we know it or not, but Bryan Kuderna's book provides a real-life guide on how to tilt the scales in your favor."

—Shawn O'Malley, Chief Editor and host at The Investor's Podcast Network

---

"You hear CFPs® give financial advice, but rarely do you learn exactly what they do with their own money every step of the way. *Simply Wealthy* was eye-opening."

—Tom Corley, bestselling author of *Rich Habits*

"Bryan Kuderna lays out a practical process to achieve wealth. This is a must-read for everyone—whether you're nervous about starting out, all the way to the ultra-wealthy. *Simply Wealthy* gives you a straightforward four-step guide to making investing work for you in any circumstance."

—Margot Machol, former Commissioner of the Federal Trade Commission and presidential advisor

---

"*Simply Wealthy* is a must-read for people who have been intimidated by financial planning. It's simple, well-written, and easy to read. Read the book, do the work, and thank Bryan when you're wealthy!"

—DAVE KERPEN, *New York Times* bestselling author of *Get Over Yourself*

"*Simply Wealthy* distills the chaos of modern finance into a clear, actionable four-step blueprint to achieve lasting financial freedom. In a marketplace flooded with noise, Bryan Kuderna offers rare clarity, discipline, and integrity—this is the kind of pragmatic money manual every CEO wishes their team, their family, and frankly their younger self had read sooner."

—*CEOWORLD MAGAZINE*

"*Simply Wealthy* is simply wonderful—a great read, packed with an actionable and common-sense approach on your journey to financial peace of mind."

—STEPHEN FOERSTER, author of *Trailblazers, Heroes, and Crooks*

"Managing your finances may not be easy, but it can be simple. *Simply Wealthy* makes personal finance as straightforward as it can be."

—SCOTT FULFORD, senior economist at the Consumer Financial Protection Bureau & author of *The Pandemic Paradox*

SIMPLY WEALTHY

THE 4-STEP PLAN FOR FINANCIAL FREEDOM

Bryan M. Kuderna, CFP®

Hatherleigh Press, Ltd.

62545 State Highway 10, Hobart, NY 13788, USA

hatherleighpress.com

Library of Congress Cataloging-in-Publication Data is available.

ISBN: 978-1-961293-58-8

Cover and interior design by Carolyn Kasper

Printed in the United States

The authorized representative in the EU for product safety and compliance is Catarina Astrom, Blästorpsvägen 14, 276 35 Borrby, Sweden.

info@hatherleighpress.com

10 9 8 7 6 5 4 3 2 1

CONTENTS

A NOTE FROM THE AUTHOR

WHAT SEPARATES MASTERS of money from those who can't seem to catch a break is the distinction between **risk capacity** (which is an objective fact) and **risk tolerance** (which is a subjective feeling). Wealthy people understand risk capacity, they are not fooled by their emotions. Unwealthy people only consider risk tolerance; they are misled by their preconceptions.

Financial planning may not be so binary as a win or lose decision, but this simple way of looking at money is what separates the haves from the have-nots. Winners tilt the odds of finance in their favor as often as possible, maximizing upside and limiting downside. It's not much different than a professional poker player seizing opportunities of high probability versus an amateur hoping for success with limited hands. This ability to objectively evaluate risk capacity in each financial decision, regardless of your risk tolerance, is built on a proven, simple, four-step financial plan.

Every year, millions of people buy books like this one because they want a clear path to become truly wealthy. But most are discarded for one reason: **a failure to inspire confidence.** The best financial advice in a mind that lacks confidence is like gold still buried in a mine, or a winning lottery ticket in the bottom of a trash can. Self-improvement books may present good ideas, good enough to highlight or share with a friend, but rarely good enough to compel permanent lifestyle changes able to resist every temptation and distraction vying for our time and money. Failure to inspire confidence and the ensuing conviction to act in one's own best interests can stem from confusion, lack of motivation, or misinformation, all of which derive from a poor source.

As the source of all that follows, you need to understand me and where I come from to have any chance at confidently following my four-step plan to financial freedom. I once heard a highly regarded surgeon tell his protégé that, "The patient doesn't need to know the plan is right, they need to know that you are right." That's why I will pull back the curtain on our sometimes puzzling industry and share my unabashed financial philosophy and experiences.

I began my career as a 21-year-old intern struggling to sell life insurance. I divulge this humbling story for two reasons. One, imagine the frame of mind of your trusted financial advisor when he or she might lose their job; then imagine how it may influence your planning conversations. It is easy for a successful entrepreneur to say never let money dictate your decisions, but it requires ample faith to uphold the code while struggling to pay your bills. In those early years of my career, I *needed* clients. When an advisor needs clients, he or she tends to want to be agreeable. A "yes-man" might give advice clients or readers *want* to hear versus what they *need* to hear. I no longer need clients; therefore, I can speak in this manual without having to be agreeable. If you are looking for professional guidance, seek an advisor who does not need your business, one who will tell you what you need to hear, not what you want to hear.

The other reason why I point out this rough stage of my career is because I understand how discouraging it is to wonder if you will be able to get by, let alone start financial planning. Not everyone starts at the same starting line, but if you are waiting for the perfect time to begin planning for your future, I can promise you that *now* is it. As I impart my advice in the coming chapters, I will disclose my own financial decisions at each stage of my life, including the very beginning. The key thing to note is that when I felt ready to plan for the future, and when I felt nowhere close to ready, it was always the right time.

Following my internship, I acquired several investment securities licenses administered by FINRA (Financial Industry Regulatory

Authority) that allowed me to begin managing money, and obtained the Certified Financial Planner™ (CFP®) designation, the standard every client should look for. Understanding the licenses of your advisors may explain why they recommend one investment versus another, a mutual fund over a stock or Exchange Traded Fund (ETF). That is not to say one solution is better than the other for a particular client, but it *can* explain why some strategies are discussed and others are not.

The public should know that every license and designation brings about a new layer of compliance. Compliance officers and regulators not only oversee what I do or say to clients and the public, they also moderate what I am allowed to do or say. This is one of the biggest reasons why a wealth manager with billions of dollars of assets under management will often go unknown, while some of the most famous financial celebrities have never managed a portfolio. The finance genre is unique in that many of its authors are not experienced in the actual dealings of finance. It is how a medical doctor can create a personal finance blog, just as I could create a healthcare forum with much greater ease than one on investing. If a blog reader mistakenly acts on their advice and goes bankrupt, the worst outcome might be some angry fan mail the blogger will probably never see. In the practicing world, a fiduciary's slightest error must be answered for.

This book will offer real-life decisions, real-life outcomes, and real-life fixes. The hypothetical laboratory is a playground for endless speculation, but the real world proves who wins and who loses. In the realm of personal finance, there is no passing the buck, you either decide what to do with your money, or your money decides what to do with you. "I didn't know" is not an excuse.

Your guide,

Bryan M. Kuderna, CFP®

INTRODUCTION

As a financial advisor, I speak face-to-face with thousands of people every year on their most intimate money matters. I'll let you in on a little industry secret: my conversations are usually about the same. Finance is way simpler than people like to make it. When I pick up the latest best-seller on personal finance or listen to a popular money guru, I am baffled by how the same timeless advice is rebranded with a new twist. I want to save you from reinventing the wheel so that you can become wealthy in the face of an uncertain future.

If you think I may be depreciating the skill of wealth management, let me clarify. I consider finance simple, but that does not mean it is easy. Exercising five times a week is simple, but most busy adults will agree that it is not easy. This feeling usually comes from a lack of discipline, a lack of enthusiasm, or both. Rarely does a day in my office go by in which a spouse or business partner does not begin a consultation with, "Talk to them, my brain just doesn't do finance." I believe this characterization is more a symptom of not wanting to know, rather than not being able to know. Don't mask laziness with supposed confusion; the truth is that financial behavior far outweighs financial intelligence. If you polled all my clients, I guarantee most view me more as a coach than a teacher.

Take one of the best-selling personal finance books of all time, *The Richest Man in Babylon* (which is just over 100 pages mind you). George S. Clason wrote this classic in 1926, so it has withstood the test of time.

Dressing up his guidance in the form of ancient sage parables, Clason espoused seven basic principles which I'll paraphrase:

1. **Start Thy Purse to Fattening:** Make money and save money.
2. **Control Thy Expenditures:** Stop wasting money.
3. **Make Thy Gold Multiply:** Invest.
4. **Guard Thy Treasures from Loss:** Don't buy every fad.
5. **Make of Thy Dwelling a Profitable Investment:** Become a homeowner.
6. **"Insure" a Future Income:** Prepare for when you will no longer be able to work.
7. **Increase Thy Ability to Earn:** Get better at making money.

There you have it—not too complicated. I know there is more to personal finance than Clason's seven blanket recommendations, just as I know pizza is more than bread, tomatoes, and cheese. My point is that anyone who wants to become a master of their money can do so, it is not an occupation reserved solely for geniuses who somehow see things differently.

A delicious pizza may only be bread, cheese, and tomatoes, but step-by-step it is perfected with the right mix of the right ingredients cooked at the right temperature at the right time. Then this is repeated day in and day out. Repeating what works matters, often this means resisting the urge to find a better way, which can be as hard as breaking a bad habit. I am sure a legendary chef is regularly tempted to tweak his staple recipe, like how a 25-year-old Tiger Woods changed the greatest golf swing ever or how Coca-Cola mistakenly created "New Coke" in 1985.

Repetition cannot rely on enthusiasm alone though. It takes discipline to repeat a truth when the world seems to tell you otherwise, same as it takes discipline not to repeat errors that the world might condone.

Discipline is what shields the process from luck and fads. Success can be dangerous in that it is not always the direct result of a sound process, just as failure is not definitive proof of a poor decision. Luck, including bad luck, is a real part of life we must all recognize. Longshots can make the totally unprepared person look like a genius, and the totally prepared person look like a fool. That's why the overarching design of this book is a simple, time-tested process thoroughly implemented on thousands of individuals from all walks of life. It is built on repetition with an unwavering goal to achieve the highest probability of success under the broadest range of circumstances.

How should you read this book? Some people go to the doctor looking for healing, are prescribed a remedy, and follow the protocol without question. If that is you, you can quickly read this book, follow the protocol, and take confidence in my experience. Other people go to the doctor looking for healing, are prescribed a remedy, and research tirelessly for the conviction to adopt the protocol or debunk it. "Prove it," they say. If that is you, you will find ample background info herein to confirm my prescriptions. Such supporting knowledge is not to make the simple complicated, but rather to prove how simple it can be.

As I write this book, there is plenty to worry about—people are recovering from the highest inflation seen in over four decades; homes have become unaffordable for many; it feels like the U.S. government is ignoring over $38 trillion of debt; millennials and Generation Z are struggling with their student loans; defined benefit pensions have almost disappeared and citizens wonder if Social Security is destined for a similar outcome; the list will always go on.

Yet with a sound and simple financial plan, this is the best time to be alive in history. The standards of living have never been higher and more widely attainable. Most of the world holds more technology and access to information in the palm of their hand than did the most elite institutions of a decade ago. The furthest-reaching luxuries of prior generations—a car, color television, a backyard pool, vacation cruises, air conditioning, sneakers designed for each sport have become commonplace.

Whether you are reading this book the day it comes out, or 50 years later, the situation will be the same: there will be issues to contend with *and* opportunities to capitalize upon. The headlines and characters may change, tomorrow's stage may look like today's science fiction, but natural human wants and needs will stay the same, and so my four steps shall remain as relevant as ever.

I am sharing this guide not just for some parts of society; it is for old and young, for risk-taking and risk-averse, for laborers and entrepreneurs. You want to know why I *really* write? I write because if financial literacy is not made universal, the wealthy are bound to watch their life's savings be pulled away by those who are not. From the plebeians and patricians of ancient Rome to today's rich and poor of the U.S.A., society has rightfully demanded that all its parts thrive.

These are my stories about what has worked and what hasn't, what I struggle with, what clients struggle with, rebuttals, objections, questions, and answers. Without further ado, here is the four-step planning process that I use every day with my clients ranging from those just getting by up to the rich and famous.

MY FINANCIAL PLANNING GOALS

IMAGINE YOUR IDEAL financial scenario, think about what a state of well-being means to you, and write down your goals on the lines below. Remember to make these S.M.A.R.T. goals—Specific, Measurable, Achievable, Relevant, and Time-bound. Defining the endgame you are working towards can serve as motivation to stay the course.

Once you have jotted down your goals, get to know your financial self with brutal honesty, let personal finance be personal. Failing to do so is a common reason why investors act out of character and damage the best-laid plans. They let their risk tolerance distort their perception of risk capacity. The four steps of my plan are universal, but understanding how you will implement them and how you will *feel* implementing them through the ups and downs of life will prepare you to maximize their results.

Short-Term (0-2 years)

1. ______________________________

2. ______________________________

3. ______________________________

Mid-Term (3-10 years)

1. ______________________________

2. ______________________________

3. ______________________________

Long-Term (10+ years)

1. ______________________________
2. ______________________________
3. ______________________________

BRYAN'S TIPS TO FINANCIAL FREEDOM:

1. Do NOT get emotional. Emotional financial decisions rarely bode well, they are often irrational. Focus on what you can control and not on what you can't.

2. A boring plan is not a bad plan. Many of life's best-laid plans are never executed because complexity provides an easy excuse to procrastinate. If you can't summarize your investment philosophy, your insurance plan, or your financial strategy in one sentence, you probably should not do it. If the plan does not make sense, then the details do not matter.

3. Avoid fads. By definition, a fad is something that is widely accepted and shared with enthusiasm, but without basis and short-lived. Strategies without basis and that are short-lived are never good strategies. This tip is not to discount new ideas and opportunities, but rather not to automatically adopt them based on recent popularity.

4. Do not be cheap. People do not shop for bargains on parachutes or brakes; so why do so with your life's savings? Naturally, all fees and rates should be warranted, efficiency is the goal, but cost is only an objection in the absence of value. When faced with an investment that has no fee and a potential 10 percent return, or one with a 1 percent fee and potential 20 percent return, a surprising amount of investors mistakenly elect the first option under the guise of getting a "deal."

5. Every opinion is valid, but so is every fact. No advisor or partner has the right to tell a person that their feelings about money are right or wrong, our feelings are our feelings. But that does not enable us to pick and choose which facts matter, facts are facts. A plan based on reality has a higher probability of success than one based on hope.

6. Stay on the same page. A common roadblock to executing the plan is when all decision makers are not singing in tune. For instance, I always make sure both spouses, all business partners, or the trusted CPA or estate attorney attend my financial planning meetings. Too often, the "financial person" shows up ready to learn and make decisions, only to then relay a message back to their spouse or partner who interjects a goal or concern that stalls the improvement.

7. DIY or don't DIY. Between the internet, artificial intelligence (AI), and other tools removing financial asymmetries, it is possible to do-it-yourself. However, many people attempt this approach only to find that life gets in the way, they get busy, they lose interest in money matters, or only focus on the parts that excite them, creating a junk drawer of financial products. Just like following one piece of the doctor's advice or only taking one medication out of the three that are prescribed can be harmful, the same goes for financial planning.

8. Be careful of your research. Many people about to embrace a new financial plan pause to "do some research" first. Similar to the last tip, the internet possesses infinite information, but not as much wisdom. It is easy to find information to build confirmation bias and support any 'yes' or 'no' answers. Just like using Dr. Google to decide whether to get a medical procedure completed or not, information should help *inform* but should not be a *substitute* for professional advice.

9. Relax your financial beliefs. Finance does not belong in the same domain as religion. Beliefs relegate an individual to being stuck where they are, unable to learn further having already pledged allegiance to a set plan or product. This is not to say that you should not stick to a plan, staying the course can be critical, but being adaptable and able to learn is equally as important. I like to say that north is north, the compass does not lie, but we must be able to change directions when the map calls for it. You are a different person than you were 10 years ago, and in 10 years you'll be a different person than you are now, as such the direction of your plans may need to change. Remember that change is not always an improvement, but an improvement is always a change.

10. There are NO maybes. A mentor of mine kept a sign in his office that said, "'Yes' is okay. 'No' is okay. But don't ever say 'maybe.'" Saying yes and saying no to each step is how you learn what works and what doesn't. Maybe's only return is lost time.

STEP 1

PROTECTION FIRST

"Don't worry. Be happy."
—Meher Baba

Your seat belt does not matter...until it matters. Then it is *all* that matters. Few people enjoy planning for the events they pray will never happen, but the alternative is to join society's growing pool of worriers. The good news is, with time on your side, most of these worries can be removed.

Risk mitigation can feel like the exact opposite of planning a vacation. But rest assured, whether it is booking that long-awaited cruise or simply purchasing a TV or your kid's new baseball bat, the transaction will be followed up with, "Would you be interested in hearing about our protection plan? Maybe some travel insurance?"

This is the point where personality meets economics. Some buyers might blindly click through any waivers in a race to their end goal, whereas others compare the potential threat with the cost of making it go away. Then there are consumers who might hear about a recent cruise cancelled due to a hurricane, or the faulty speaker on the TV, or the grip that tends to peel off the baseball bat, and completely abandon the transaction for fear of all these possible issues.

None of these reactions and ensuing decisions are right or wrong, until they are right or wrong for *you*.

FAILURE TO PREPARE MEANS PREPARING TO FAIL

Preparation, like risk tolerance, is subjective. For example, a car that breaks down after 10 years might be an accepted eventuality for one driver and a disaster for another. Adequate preparation can be defined as avoiding a negative surprise; that is the only true responsibility of risk mitigation. Once the potential fallouts and various contingency plans are fully disclosed, it is solely up to the individual to decide which measures are worthwhile and which are not.

The important things to know are:

- The full extent of financial exposure.
- The costs of protection.
- The value of the cost and value of the loss.

The customer who bought the protection plan for their TV has no right to complain about wasted money when it works perfectly forever, just as the person who forgoes the plan has no right to complain when its speaker pops after just six months.

Assuming full transparency and an understanding of thyself, there are three popular reasons why families and businesses can still be left unprepared for moments when everyone else says, "How could they have let this happen?"

1. The preparation is a boring inconvenience.
2. It requires admitting vulnerability (and, for the superstitious, manifests bad juju).
3. It is confusing.

The first excuse is a form of laziness, which we are all susceptible to, depending on the intensity of the preparation and the magnitude of the foreseeable gain or loss. The second excuse is illogical, a symptom of hubris or a disconnect with statistics. The third excuse, confusion, may be more to blame on the industry than the public (and is likely why you are reading this book).

But there is one more reason why gaping holes can be found in plans designed with the best intentions...**cost.** Spending money on something one wants is easily justifiable, even with a generous margin for overspending. An extra thousand dollars for the family vacation of a lifetime can be overlooked. The expected result is an enjoyable one; the focus is on the end, not the means. However, spending money on something one never wants to experience goes against the grain of human nature, eliminating the margin for overspending by a penny. The focus is on the means, not the end.

The differences between cost and price were introduced in my previous book, *What Should I Do with My Money?*, to make sense of economic decisions on the grandest of scales. The same concept applies to personal risk management. Price is the quantifiable amount paid for something. It is the metric that creates a marketplace for all services and goods. In terms of risk management, if one insurance policy is priced at $99 and another is priced at $100, holding all things equal, purchase the one for $99 every time, all the time.

However, cost does not hold all things equal. Cost acknowledges the countless variables beyond price. Price is irrespective of value; it is purely a number. Cost is only an objection in the absence of value; it is a combination of price, time, enjoyment, pain, and lost opportunity costs all in exchange for a desired outcome. The price of the insurance policy may be $99 or $100, but the cost is this outlay plus the inconvenience of research, planning, acknowledging vulnerabilities, forgoing other fun expenditures, and ultimately its usefulness when needed most.

To determine the appropriate means to an end, the focus should start at the end and work backwards. What does the end, the desired result, look like? This is unique to every situation. Furthermore, there is not one finish line to strive for; life is an amalgamation of countless ends. The end can be to buy a first house, put the kids through college, retire at age 60, sell a business, leave a legacy to grandchildren or a favorite charity, pay off student loans, etc. The list is endless and different for each individual, family, or business.

Visualizing this optimal chain of events should be done with attention to detail. Babe Ruth did not just visualize hitting a game-winning homerun; he visualized the pitcher's wind-up, his release, the spin on the ball approaching him, the shift of his weight and rotating hips, the barrel of his bat colliding with the ball, the follow-through, and then watching the baseball soar over the centerfield fence.

Why is Step 1: Protection First, so easily overlooked? Even when the end has been defined and one begins working backwards to today; what does it take to get the car, the house, the retirement, or the vacation? It takes money. So, one logically tallies up the price of their desired ends, determines if the costs are worth the result, and then begins accumulating. People rush to those ends, straight to Step 4: Wealth Maximization. If the world worked perfectly all the time, Step 4 might be the only step, but that's not the world we live in, there are traps along the way.

"Plan for the future. Start investing now," the worn-out boss implores his junior workers.

"Just max out your retirement plan as soon as you can, don't end up working forever like me," the mother tells her child.

"Fund a college savings plan the day that baby is born," says the parent still paying off their own student loans.

Are these not all noble pieces of advice everyone should be following? Of course they are, but in due time. Visualizing the sum and reverse engineering the addition to get there makes sense in the laboratory, but can spell disaster in the real world. The real world is wrought with pitfalls, changes, adversaries, and much more. In short, the real world is not just pluses and multiplications, but carries minuses and divisions that are often hidden in the shadows.

Lurking in those shadows are mistakes, sometimes purely the result of confusion. Many people are proactive and recognize "it could happen to me," but then are baffled by over-information. I often say in my seminars that in the world of finance, "I didn't know" is not an excuse. *But that's not fair.* No, it is not, but that is reality. The rest of this chapter aims to remove such confusion.

Financial planning is no different than any other preparation in that its value is derived from two sources. First, the creation of positive pathways; and second, the removal of negative pathways. Recall that one of my "Tips to Financial Freedom" is: **Do NOT get emotional.** Well-protected plans offer the financial benefit of assuring the most efficient positive pathways, but also the emotional benefit of removing negative ones. Financial decisions and emotional decisions are two different sides of the same coin. Step 1: Protection First does not generate positive pathways by itself nor the positive emotions that accompany growing wealth, but like the seatbelt resting across your chest, it is ready to save the day when called upon. This removes negative pathways; it removes worry. It can protect an aggressive investor or entrepreneur from their own ambitions and give the conservative miser the confidence to take advantage of opportunities otherwise deemed too risky. Proper protection can empower people to follow Meher Baba's saying, popularized later by Bob Marley, "Don't worry. Be happy." You can't fully have one without the other.

STEP 1A: INSURE FUTURE CASH FLOW

Disability Insurance

What is the first step of the first step—Step 1A? Every financial plan starts with income (not counting people who made it the old-fashioned way of inheriting it). During the accumulation phase of life, work creates cash flow, which covers everything from daily living expenses to buying real estate and businesses up to funding a retirement and legacy plan. In the decumulation phase, commonly retirement, assets are converted back into cash flow to continue living a comfortable life.

I begin most of my client relationships by asking, "What are the three things you most want to accomplish?" You could be the serial entrepreneur chasing fortunes, or the worker wanting a debt free life with a guaranteed retirement income. Look back at your list of goals and think about the financial costs to each one. No matter what your vision board looks like, it is going to take money, which either comes from income or came from income.

Disability Income Insurance is the best way to secure the positive pathways that make up one's goals. Why is it so often ignored, then? Consumers readily accept buying auto insurance, homeowners insurance, jewelry insurance, cell phone insurance, even warranties on relatively small purchases like headphones. Each of these items represents its own end. Earned income is not an end; it is not tangible, it is purely the means to the desired ends, and therefore difficult to grasp and want to fully protect. People are conditioned to insure their golden eggs but not the goose laying those eggs.

"I really wanted this new sports car. I've worked and saved so long for this dream; I'm insuring it to the max."

It is an obvious conclusion: protect the thing you have earned. In 2016, Michael Phelps, arguably the greatest athlete ever with a record 23 gold medals, summed it up well. He appeared on *The Ellen DeGeneres*

Show, and Ellen asked him how he protects his priceless medals, "Are the medals just hidden? Like in a safe, I would hope, or something?"

Phelps responded, "They're in a secret place, where there are probably two people in the world who know where they are."

"Where?" Ellen tried again.

"You're not one of the two people," Phelps politely shut her down.

The point is, imagine if before making Olympic history, Phelps lost his ability to swim. The world over would not recognize his name, let alone wonder where the secret vault is that houses all his gold. For someone like a world-class athlete who has spent their life perfecting such a singular skill—swimming, hitting a golf ball, or throwing a 100 mile-per-hour fastball, a career-ending injury is the most heartbreaking occasion in sports.

For those whom my kids call NARPs (non-athletic regular people), also known as the 99.9 percent of us who work every day, we have the ability to remove the "what ifs" our favorite athletes so greatly fear. When I ask a client what their goals are, their financial gold medals, we will come up with a plan to achieve them, and then protect them once they are attained. But first, we will protect the pathways to get there, insuring their skillset to work and earn an income, securing their ability to swim from point A to point B.

You may be digesting these sports analogies and say to yourself, "Well, if Tom Brady could have insured his career when he was 22 years old, wouldn't it have been way more important during his rookie year than during his last year with the Tampa Bay Buccaneers, when his legacy was already cemented?"

Certainly true. But in the NARP world, remember that life is an amalgamation of ends. The young professional may view their income as a means to pay for a wedding and buy their first house. But then, in his or her prime, it may be to buy a bigger house and help their kids pay for college. Then, in the twilight of their career, it may be to fund retirement so they can travel the world and leave a bequest to their grandkids. The series of ends has a series of pathways. So yes, disability income insurance is arguably more important for the young professional than the person approaching retirement, but someone banking on working to age 65 likely would not be too happy to be forced to exit at age 60. If there is another year to work, then there is an economic value worth protecting, just like a future hall-of-famer taking one last run at a Super Bowl.

If you have read this far, the first excuse about being too lazy to plan probably does not apply to you. So, what about the second one—vulnerability and perception versus reality? Most healthy individuals, especially young professionals, do not think they will ever become too sick or injured to work. However, according to the Social Security Administration (SSA), more than one in four 20-year-olds will become disabled before reaching retirement age.

The reality is that most disabilities don't look like what people think of when they hear the word "disabled." People envision the horrific car accident that leaves someone paralyzed. While that is possible, and tens of thousands of motor vehicle accidents happen every day in the U.S., there are many more likely causes.

The most common reasons for long-term disability claims are:

- Musculoskeletal disorders (27.6 percent)
- Cancer (15 percent)
- Injuries (12 percent)
- Mental health issues (9.3 percent)
- Circulatory issues like heart attack and stroke (8.2 percent)[1]

[1] Integrated Benefits Institute, Health and Productivity Benchmarking 2019 (released September 2020), Long-Term Disability, All Employers. Condition-specific results. https://files.ibiweb.org/uploads/general/Sample-Reports.zip

Whenever I give a lecture on this topic, there will always be at least one female in the audience who will say, "What about pregnancy?" It is a great point that leads into an area that is easily confused. There are ultimately two types of disability insurance: long-term and short-term. Pregnancy is the #1 cause of short-term disability claims, followed by musculoskeletal disorders, injuries, digestive disorders, and mental health issues, respectively.[2] There is an overlap present as musculoskeletal disorders, injuries, and mental health issues can often begin as a short-term claim that does not resolve, and which morphs into a long-term claim.

Fortunately, most pregnancies, and even complicated pregnancies, never reach the long-term qualification. To clarify, short-term disability plans typically begin paying benefits one to two weeks after a qualifying injury or illness and last for three to six months, or until you are able to return to work. Long-term disability benefits typically begin 90 days (sometimes 180 days) after the qualifying illness or injury and will usually pay to age 65 or age 67.

This might be a good time to caution readers against the frequency illusion, sometimes referred to as recency bias. People often buy or do not buy disability insurance based on anecdotal evidence. They recently learned of someone who broke their leg skiing, was out of work for a complicated pregnancy, or was diagnosed with cancer. Whatever the story may be, it is easy to then think that that is the most likely or even only outcome. Good protection plans rely on statistics and all possibilities, not just ones that may appear frequent.

"Makes sense, but I'm pretty sure I'm already covered."

Disability insurance is often an assumed benefit.

[2] Integrated Benefits Institute, Health and Productivity Benchmarking 2019 (released September 2020), Short-Term Disability, All Employers. Condition-specific results. https://files.ibiweb.org/uploads/general/Sample-Reports.zip.

There are three reasons uncovered workers mistakenly think they are covered:

1. **Health Insurance:** There is a "medical" or "health" deduction on every paystub; it was even mandated nationwide by the Affordable Care Act (ACA). While health insurance addresses the same issues of illness and injuries, it is typically limited to the treatment thereof (i.e., hospital stays, doctor's bills, prescriptions, examinations, and procedures, etc.). It has nothing to do with protecting income.
2. **Social Security:** The government, Social Security Disability Insurance (SSDI), has its own program for American workers. However, SSDI uses a very strict definition in which to qualify, the claimant must suffer a severe medical condition expected to last at least one year or result in death. Furthermore, it must prevent the claimant from doing work they did in the past and adjusting to any other work in the future. Even if the claimant has such a catastrophic disability that qualifies, the maximum SSDI benefit in 2025 is $4,018 monthly.[3]
3. **Coverage Through Work:** This is another convoluted issue, one involving Workers' Compensation and Group Disability Insurance. Workers' Compensation only covers an illness or injury that is directly work-related or happened while on the job. Group coverage may automatically cover employees, especially at larger companies, but it often comes with several drawbacks. These can include a lack of portability (leave the job, leave the coverage), benefits offsetting for other income sources, definitions that require the worker

[3] Social Security Administration

to be unable to perform any gainful employment, lack of inflation protection or partial disability coverage, and benefit amounts that may only cover a fraction of the worker's normal income.

Through reasons #2 and #3, many workers are correct in identifying as already covered. The conclusion is that not all coverage is created equal, and the best coverage is the one that pays the most when you need it the most.

The most effective method to protect a financial plan from disability is to use an individually owned, non-cancellable, guaranteed renewable true own-occupation policy. Allow me to simplify this tongue twister. "Individually owned" means the person owns the policy themselves, not an employer or association. "Noncancellable" means the insurance carrier cannot cancel, increase the premiums, or reduce the benefits, so long as the owner pays their premium. "Guaranteed renewable" means the owner can continue to renew their plan with the same terms every year. "True-own occupation" means the carrier must approve the disability claim if the insured cannot perform the material and substantial duties of their own occupation; benefits will not be reduced even if working in another occupation.

Someone shopping for individual disability insurance has three levers they can pull: contract language, benefits, and price. They can find the largest monthly benefit amount with the longest benefit period at the lowest price if they are willing to sacrifice the contract language (i.e. buying an Any Occupation definition that will only pay if the insured is unable to perform any occupation). Whereas someone looking for the best contract language at the lowest price will likely have to settle for a smaller benefit amount or benefit period.

There is one more lever that can supersede all of these—the quality of the carrier. Like any guarantee in finance, a "guarantee" may be better understood as a "promise." U.S. Treasuries are widely recognized as the safest investment in the world, backed by the full faith and credit of the United States government, but even this acknowledges a condition, in that the full faith and credit of the U.S. government remains solvent. An insurer may list an array of benefits for the insured throughout a 100-page disability insurance contract, but these "promises" are guaranteed when the carrier is able to fulfill its obligations years or decades down the road. One of the best ways to analyze an insurance carrier's creditworthiness is by researching their Comdex score, which is a combination of multiple rating services such as A.M. Best, Fitch, Moody's, and Standard & Poor's. Mutual carriers, those that are entirely owned by their policyholders, often have a higher Comdex score than stock companies, which are owned by outside shareholders paying closer attention to quarterly earnings reports.

Top-rated carriers tend to be stricter in their medical underwriting process, reinforcing the idea of locking in coverage while young and healthy. If you are wondering what reasons prevent a carrier from granting approval, look back at the top causes of disability outlined earlier. They are the claims costing insurance carriers hundreds of millions of dollars every year in benefits to disabled clients, and as such, receive extra scrutiny. Furthermore, the type of occupation plays a large role; a poorly recovered hand fracture is going to garner more attention from an underwriter for a surgeon than it would for an accountant. The best plans are akin to an exclusive club, in that once inside, you will be well taken care of, but getting through the door is not available to everyone. This is why locking in Individual Disability Income Insurance while young and healthy is so time-sensitive.

WHAT DID I DO?

As a young professional, my vision board was made up of a thriving business, big house, nice car, and happy family. Like most people, I saw the ends, not the means, and certainly not protecting those means. It was not until I was 27 years old that I purchased an Individual Non-Cancellable Guaranteed Renewable Own Occupation policy. Not terribly old, but for someone who started in the business at 21 years old, it was obviously not my first move—which was a mistake.

I paid a price for my tardiness. Not only is the policy costing me more every year for the rest of my career versus had I obtained it five years or so sooner (the cost is based on the age you start at), but I also have a medical exclusion on my policy that would not have been present just a couple of years before I applied.

I prided myself on staying in peak shape through exercise and diet and even completed a full Ironman just three months before getting my policy. However, about two years before I decided to protect my income, the week I was to be the best man at my buddy's wedding, I suddenly had a terrible pain from my throat down to my upper chest. Within hours, I could not swallow any food, and shortly thereafter, taking a sip of water was excruciating. With no medical history or preexisting conditions whatsoever, I immediately had an endoscopy performed, which showed my esophagus to be extremely ulcerated. Biopsies were inconclusive, and within a few days I felt fine and was able to make my friend's wedding. The gastrointestinal physician could not explain it, and even asked if I may have accidentally swallowed Draino or some other poison-like substance. In summary, I still got the best health rating and full benefits from the highest-rated insurance carrier, but with an exclusion for my esophagus, which is on my policy to this day.

So, why did I wait roughly five or six years into my career to pull the trigger? First, it took a couple of years to build my financial services practice to a level that provided an income worth insuring. Second, like many of my friends in their 20s, I was invincible, even the random esophagus scare two years prior did not provide any motivation for me to get protected.

I had thought a lot about disability insurance from an economic standpoint, by virtue of designing financial plans for many families and businesses. I knew all the statistics. I knew that disability was one of the leading causes of bankruptcy and home foreclosures every year. I knew it was the perfect storm of lost income mixed with healthcare costs, family strain, and more.

I vividly remember a very successful veteran of our industry telling me that, "Financial planning is all about trading big mistakes for little mistakes. If you pay two percent of your income throughout your career for disability insurance," he went on to say, "and wake up healthy the day you retire having never used it, then financially speaking, that was a little mistake. But!" he started to get emotional, "If you decide to cheap out on a disability policy, and then someday, with a mortgage, with a family, with a business all depending on you, you suddenly wake up and you're not the healthy kid you once were, and you get sick and can't go do your job, now it's a huge mistake!" I got it. But I didn't get *it*.

One time I brought an old mentor of mine along for a financial literacy presentation at a hospital. I let him take the disability part of the lecture. He shared a story spur of the moment that I'd never heard before...

"Let me tell you about one of my best clients. He is the managing partner at one of the top law firms on the East Coast. Since the first day he started investing with me, I began telling him about the importance of getting disability insurance. He'd casually brush it aside, but I kept reminding him at each of our annual reviews.

'Howard,' he said to me, 'I understand you're just doing your job, but I've told you it's not something I'm interested in.'

'This firm is counting on you,' I replied, 'and you have almost a seven-figure income, and live a seven-figure lifestyle with your wife and son.'

'Look,' he said, 'I'm a health nut. I run a marathon every year. I work out every morning before I come in. Heck, even if you took my legs out from under me, I'd be here the next day in a wheelchair, still practicing law because I love what I do.'

I figured it was a lost cause and decided it was time to stop bringing it up. He was a great client and we had a great relationship. Then, when I least expected it, at one of our reviews, he randomly said, 'You think I should still get that disability insurance?'

'Why, what's wrong?' I immediately asked.

'Nothing at all, but you've been good to me these years, and if it's something you really believe in, then let's do it.'

I placed an enormous policy on him, a perfect rating, no health history, all good. About two years after I sold him that policy, his wife called my office out of the blue.

'Howard?'

'Yes.'

'Did you ever end up doing a disability plan with my husband?'

'Yes.'

'I think we need to talk about it.'

I was taken aback, of all my clients, this was Superman, I couldn't have imagined anything too bad. 'Why, what's up?' I asked her.

'Well,' her voice shuddered, 'our son was killed in a car accident two months ago, and he hasn't gone back into the office since.'

Silence. I couldn't find the words to say.

We began the claims process. My client was in a deep depression, and guiding his law firm was nowhere near his mind. As a mental/nervous disorder, that claim paid, and continued to pay for almost two years until he was mentally ready to return to work and focus on his firm."

That day, I went to a seminar looking to educate and hopefully pick up some new clients. But at that moment, I made up my mind. I was already financially vested, but now I was emotionally vested. I drove back to my office and filled out an application for disability insurance.

FREQUENTLY ASKED QUESTIONS

How much coverage should I have?

Answer: How much *income* would you like to have? Some people tend to settle for some coverage, meeting the task halfway. They try to justify this decision by hoping a disability never happens. **No reasonable worker would purposefully negotiate for a lower salary, so be careful not to do this with your income protection.** Realize it or not, every dollar in every budget is accounted for, whether it goes towards daily living, investing, saving, charity, or frivolous spending, it all goes somewhere, and so it is best to protect as many of those dollars as possible.

Most disability insurance plans are quoted by monthly benefit amount, but do not let this breakdown belittle your overall earning potential. For instance, a 30-year-old making a $100,000 salary with a three percent annual raise working until age 67 is on pace to earn over $6.5 million in their career. Most carriers will protect up to 60 percent of your earned income. Group Long-Term Disability may cover 40–60 percent up to a monthly benefit limit (e.g. $2,000 monthly or $10,000 monthly). Some policies will offset for other benefits or income, whereas Individual True Own Occupation coverage does not offset for other sources. When applying for individual coverage, it is important to fully disclose your income and any other disability insurance in force so as to avoid over insurance that could cause discrepancies should a disability claim occur.

Are disability insurance benefits taxable?

Answer: Possibly. Workman's compensation is generally not taxed at the federal or state level. Social Security Disability Insurance may be taxable if your yearly income is over certain thresholds. Group disability insurance can be taxable if it is employer-paid, unless the employer "grosses-up" the employee's income to cover the premium. It can also be tax-free if the employee pays for it with after-tax dollars. Individual disability insurance benefits are generally received income tax-free if the insured paid their premiums with post-tax dollars.

I can protect my income from disability, but what about some of the debts I owe or the investments I make?

Answer: Many carriers offer riders to cover specific liabilities, such as student loans, business loans, and business overhead expenses, to help cover such bills without using up base disability benefits. Some policies can also cover investment contributions, such as funding retirement plans. This is an important feature as many disabled persons who are on claim are not active participants in a retirement plan and live in fear of the day when their disability benefits stop, typically at age 65 or 67. Being able to not only cover ordinary income but also satisfy liabilities and plan for retirement, should be the goal.

How long should my benefit period be for?

Answer: The average disability lasts almost three years.[4] Remember that short-term disability typically provides benefits for three to six months. Long-term disability can be purchased for various benefit periods ranging from two or five years out to age 65 or further. It is generally considered best to insure your projected working career, knowing that the policy can always be reduced or cancelled if self-insurance eventually becomes possible. But just like people working in their sixties are not working for free, income at that age may still be critical.

[4] Council for Disability Awareness, The Average Duration of Long-Term Disability is 31.2 Months (Jan. 2016), https://blog. disabilitycanhappen.org/the-average-duration-of-long-term-disability-is-31-2-months

Should I increase my coverage as my income goes up?
Answer: Definitely yes. The best carrier, definition, and benefit period do not mean very much if it only covers your starting salary from 20 years ago, especially if you are now earning 10 times that. Many policies come with an increase option that will allow the policy owner to add more coverage without further medical underwriting to keep up with their current pay. All the more reason to lock it in while young and healthy.

Why would I ever buy an Any Occupation definition when True Own Occupation is available?
Answer: One reason is that Any Occupation policies are almost always cheaper. By definition, they are meant to pay claims less often by requiring severe injuries or illnesses that preclude the insured from doing any job, fitting the adage that, "You get what you pay for." The other common reason is that there are fewer True Own Occupation policies in the marketplace, and such carriers typically require more stringent medical underwriting. Therefore, applicants who are older, have any health issues, and/or engage in what could be considered riskier occupations are less likely to be approved for True Own Occupation policies.

STEP 1B: INSURE FUTURE CASH FLOW

Life Insurance

Disability and job loss can be a traumatic enough combination to make one quip, "Just put me out of my misery." Sometimes this happens, disabilities can lead to death, and other times death comes without any warning. The reality is that at some point in life, every human either becomes 100 percent dependent on someone else or dies suddenly. The only difference is how long the dependency lasts and how much advance notice there is before one's end.

Steps 1A and 1B can so far make this book look like the most depressing one in the library, but acknowledging the two greatest threats to income loss is part of a responsible financial plan. The future can't be told, but it can be prepared for. All this chapter is asking is that you lock the door at night.

Life insurance is arguably the safest and most efficient way to transfer wealth from one person to another. The cool thing about life insurance is that it is not only a loss preventer—it can also be a win multiplier, playing into Steps 1, 2, and 4 simultaneously. It can salvage the worst kind of financial loss when a breadwinner or partner passes away unexpectedly, or it can multiply a lifetime of savings to be left to future generations. Both short-term and long-term considerations are needed to fairly evaluate this product.

The efficiency of a policy, cost versus benefit, is dictated by three primary factors: age, health, and gender. The time-sensitive nature of obtaining life and disability insurance is another reason why these steps are 1A and 1B. The older the applicant is, the more expensive the same benefit will be. Add in a new diagnosis or medical condition, and available options can quickly become inferior, if not all gone.

"I'm making a lot of money; can't I just self-insure?"

Before delving into the specifics of life insurance, let's consider if it is possible to self-insure. People tend to fall into the trap of seeing their portfolio or their savings and taking comfort that, if something bad did occur, there is a decent sum of money to get the job done. But what *is* that job? Most accounts are already earmarked for some other goal or concern—college tuition, retirement, a vacation home, a new car, for the grandkids, etc. The list goes on.

If you were frugal enough to save 10 percent of your income every year, with no earmarks, just for the real rainy day, it would only take missing one year of work to cancel out those 10 hard years of saving. To echo the earlier disability conversation, imagine if it were two years or five years of missed work. In the life insurance conversation, permanently lost income is a guarantee.

People nearing retirement or already retired can make a stronger case for self-insurance if their balance sheet is strong and there is no longer a need for further earned income. "I've got nothing left to give," the retiree says. Yes, but you still have a lot you hope to take. Again, those accounts are for something—vacations, gifts to grandkids, taxes, healthcare, etc. As they are used and depleted throughout this decumulation phase, funds intended to continue a comfortable lifestyle for a widow or left as a legacy may erode.

In both phases, accumulation and decumulation, the replacement power of life insurance remains. To secure a multitude of lifetime goals and post-mortem goals, it can require a very high savings rate and corresponding investment returns to equal an income-tax-free life insurance death benefit. The question, then, is this: are the efforts of such a savings rate, volatility, and investment risks preferred over outsourcing the need for life insurance? As idle money defeats the purpose of wealth in motion, these enormous reserves can be recaptured through appropriate plans.

Once life insurance enters the financial plan, buyers may initially think this is one of the simpler purchases. If you die, they pay your family, pretty black and white. However, the four levers mentioned in shopping for disability insurance (contract language, benefit, price, and quality of carrier) exist here too. Here is a guideline in bite-size portions to make the process easier to navigate:

#1: DECIDING ON HOW MUCH BENEFIT

This should be the first question to ask. An affordable policy with the best terms through a premier carrier won't mean much if it leaves a widow or orphan poor. Where figuring out the right amount of disability insurance is more apparent (continue one's expected income), calculating the appropriate death benefit can be more complex. The industry follows a standard called *Human Life Value* (HLV), which is a multiple of age and income. The generally accepted maximum amount of coverage available from ages 18 through 40 is 30x income, 20x in the 40s, 15x income in the 50s, and then geared toward retirement and estate planning thereafter. This should provide the economic value to a family or business to carry on financially as if the deceased person continued to work their career.

"But my spouse works full-time, too, and makes almost the same salary I do."

This is a common line of reasoning for acquiring a lower amount of death benefit. It is the 21st century, and many households have dual incomes. Could they get by? They could. Perhaps for a couple without children or dependents, if the widow cuts expenses to suit one income, downsizes, and continues working unimpeded.

I have referenced the "laboratory" and the "real world" already and will continue to do so because we are not robots. Financial consequences have emotional consequences, and emotional consequences have financial consequences. Often, when a loved one passes away, even if they are not the breadwinner, there is an immediate shock to the financial plan. This is not referring to burial and funeral expenses that can be a temporary hit, but rather the emotional toll that can interrupt work and life. This can be amplified for a family with children, as it unsettles their situation and causes a chain reaction requiring a working parent to work less and parent more. So yes, they could get by, but the best financial plans do not settle for just getting by.

#2: CHOOSING THE RIGHT TYPE

This decision is the most debated one. There are two basic types of life insurance—**term** and **permanent**. Term life insurance is meant to be temporary coverage for a specific period of years; a 20-year term is a popular choice. If the insured dies within the term, their beneficiaries will receive the death benefit income tax-free. Checking the box with the cheapest option possible often lands here. However, many studies show that roughly 99 percent of all term policies never pay a claim.[5] This is good news in that if an applicant is healthy enough to get approved, they can have a high level of confidence that they will outlive their term. Term insurance serves strictly as a loss preventer.

Many term policies offer a conversion privilege that allows the insured to convert their coverage into a permanent policy without having to go through medical underwriting again. This can leave the door open to adapt to life changes and remove the feeling that each year that passes was money spent for nothing. Permanent policies come in many different forms; their aim is to be a win multiplier. Here is a summary of each, but due to the countless ways to structure and fit them in a financial plan, it is best coordinated specifically with your financial advisor.

Whole Life Insurance:[6]

Whole Life insurance is the longest-standing and most popular life insurance product. In 2024, life insurance sales topped $15.9 billion, according to LIMRA's U.S. Life Insurance Sales Survey. Whole Life represented 36 percent of the market share at $5.8 billion.[7] Whole

[5] https://www.thezebra.com/resources/research/life-insurance-statistics

[6] All whole life insurance policy guarantees are subject to the timely payment of all required premiums and the claims-paying ability of the issuing insurance company. Policy loans and withdrawals affect the guarantees by reducing the policy's death benefit and cash values. Some whole life policies do not have cash values in the first two years of the policy and don't pay a dividend until the policy's third year. Talk to your financial representative and refer to your individual whole life policy illustration for more information. Dividends are not guaranteed and are declared annually by the carrier.

[7] https://www.limra.com/en/newsroom/news-releases/2024/u.s.-life-insurance-premium-sets-new-record-in-2023

Life offers a guaranteed level premium, can be guaranteed to be paid up at a specific age or after a set timeframe, and has a permanent income tax-free Death Benefit that grows at a guaranteed rate with potential dividends. Dividends can be left to compound and accelerate the growth of the policy, can be used to offset premium payments, or can be received as cash. Many policies can contain a Long-Term Care feature or accelerated benefit rider that allows the insured to advance their death benefit while alive when chronically or terminally ill, and a disability waiver of premium that waives the premium if the insured were to become disabled. Lastly, Whole Life contains an accessible Cash Value that grows tax-deferred at a guaranteed rate plus potential dividends.

The growth of Cash Value can be broken down into four stages.

1. **Early Years:** Initially, premium payments will exceed cash value growth.
2. **Positive Net Cash Flow:** This is when the annual increase in net cash value exceeds the annual net premium. Depending on how the policy is structured, this can begin around policy years 5–8.
3. **Net Cash Value Exceeds Cumulative Premium:** This is the year in which the policy has more cash value than has been paid in all years' premiums. This can occur around policy years 10–14, depending on the structure and dividend history.
4. **Self-Supporting Policy:** There may now be enough dividends to pay the full annual premium going forward.

Indexed Universal Life (IUL):[8]

This is a relatively new product that accounts for 24 percent or $3.8 billion of market share. It is a permanent type of life insurance that relies on a crediting rate typically tied to an external index, most commonly the S&P 500. Since premiums are not actually invested, the crediting rate offers a floor (e.g. 0 percent) when the index posts a negative return, but a cap on the upside (e.g. 10 percent). This sounds attractive, investment potential without the investment risk, but unlike Whole Life, IUL policies have several non-guaranteed variables which include changing cap rates, policy charges, participation rates in the underlying indexes, and even the premium. Universal Life Insurance may lapse prematurely due to inadequate funding, an increase in the cost of insurance rates as the insured grows older, and a low interest crediting rate.

Variable Universal Life (VUL)

This represents 14 percent of total U.S. life insurance sales or $2.2 billion. It is similar to IUL, but can expose the insured to loss based on the investment funds chosen. This adds more risk in that if the cost of insurance increases at the same time the stock market drops, the insured may have to pay additional premiums or incur a lapse.

[8] An Indexed Universal Life (IUL) policy is not considered a security. Premium and death benefit types are flexible. Its crediting rate is based on the performance of a stock index with a cap rate (e.g. 10 percent), a floor (e.g. 0 percent), and a participation rate (e.g., 100 percent). This type of universal life policy may lapse due to low or negative performance of the stock index, inadequate funding, and increasing cost of insurance rates.

Fixed Universal Life (UL)

The smallest of the permanent products, totaling $1.1 billion in 2024 or 7 percent market share, this does not have an investment component or tie to any stock index, but receives an annual interest credit. For this reason, it may be seen as a conservative alternative to IUL or VUL. Like IUL and VUL, Fixed Universal Life is often marketed as a "flexible premium" product that gives the owner the option to pay more or less as needed; however, it works both ways, as the carrier can raise rates in the future.

Disclosure: I personally have only sold Term, Whole Life, and Guaranteed Universal Life. In other words, I have never in my career used a VUL or IUL for any of my clients or myself. While I am licensed to sell all these products, it has been my philosophy to avoid taking on risk inside the practice of risk management. ULs, by nature, have several nonguaranteed components that can work against the insured over the long term. The handful of Guaranteed ULs I have used were for very specific purposes in unique estate plans or as required by lenders for business loans. VULs and IULs exacerbate this unpredictability by introducing additional variables and the element of stock market risk. I much prefer the predictability of Level Term and Whole Life to satisfy the goals of risk management.

#3: QUALITY OF CARRIER

The same considerations discussed previously about disability insurance apply here. The financial strength of an insurance company can be even more important when looking into permanent insurance. Its performance, be it dividends in a Whole Life policy or the variable costs and crediting rates in a Universal Life policy, is dependent on the carrier's future.

#4: COST

Price is not the concern; it should always be the more comprehensive metric of cost. Knowing that term life insurance only lasts for so long, the death benefit does not grow, and it offers no cash value or potential dividends, why not purchase Whole Life? The answer is price. A 30-year-old female in average health could buy a $1 million 20-Year Level Term policy for roughly $40–$50 monthly. The price for the same young lady to buy a $1 million Whole Life policy could reach $1,000 monthly. Someone looking for the benefits of Whole Life, but without the budget ready for such a commitment, could obtain a Convertible Term Life policy locked in at their current age and health that is able to convert to Whole Life in the future, or a blend of Whole Life and Term that meets their Human Life Value needs.

"Why not just buy term and invest the difference?"

This is the most popular objection to buying Whole Life. Take the example just mentioned, the young lady could buy her $1 million Term policy for $50 monthly or $600 annually and invest the approximately $11,400 difference. Over the course of 20 years, she would have had a $1 million death benefit and hypothetically contributed $228,000 to her investments. When she turns 50, her death benefit would drop to $0, but assuming a 5 percent net after-tax rate of return, she would have roughly $380,000 in her portfolio (subject to capital gains taxes, or income taxes inside of a pretax qualified retirement plan). Now, if she had done the $1 million Whole Life policy, at the end of 20 years, she would have roughly $1.26 million income tax-free death benefit and $308,000 cash value, both continuing to grow at their slow and steady rate.

It is not that one approach is better than the other; only time can have the ultimate say, but rather that both have pros and cons. The term/invest proponent might suggest the young lady could pass away a year later at 31 years old after making just $600 of premium payments versus

$12,000 (granted, both scenarios would yield astronomical returns with a $1 million tax-free proceed). Or, she thinks that the markets could go on a great run and produce an 8 percent average net return instead of 5 percent. Both valid points.

The Whole Life proponent is entitled to as many, if not more, hypotheticals. The stock market crashes in her 19th policy year, wiping out much of the investor's portfolio, where her cash value continues to increase. She passes away at 51 years old, and the investor leaves behind only what's left in her portfolio versus the Whole Life's over $1 million tax-free death benefit. She gets disabled at 40 years old, and stops contributing entirely to her investments, whereas the Whole Life policy continues to be funded indefinitely by the company. She decides to continue her life insurance past 50 to secure their kids' college bills, or as a tool to replace lost Social Security benefits or a depleted 401(k) for her spouse in retirement, or to meet newfound legacy goals for grandchildren, only to find coverage is now significantly more expensive or unattainable because of a medical condition. Perhaps, after some market turmoil, she decides investing in equities is too uncomfortable and resets to a low-risk/low-reward portfolio.

The takeaway is that equities and Whole Life are two different financial vehicles. A Whole Life owner should not compare their cash value returns to the stock market. Conversely, an investor should not compare the volatility and emotional roller coaster of equities with the security of Whole Life. A financial plan should not have one or the other, but both. The guarantees, tax advantages, and ability to repurpose Whole Life throughout your whole life (pun intended), can offer added certainty, which can help an investor be a more confident investor.[9]

[9] All scenarios and names mentioned herein are purely fictional and have been created solely for educational purposes. Any resemblance to existing situations, persons or fictional characters is coincidental. The information presented should not be used as the basis for any specific investment advice.

WHAT DID I DO?

As a finance major and economics minor in college, I learned a lot about the stock market. I learned absolutely nothing about insurance. For that reason, I had aspirations of graduating, making money, and quickly investing in equities to build my fortune. Like most young professionals, I was encouraged to pursue Step 4: Wealth Maximization without any regard for Steps 1–3. I was a product of the academic laboratory, and not the real world. After I completed my internship and learned about insurance, my attitude shifted.

I purchased my first life insurance policy at 22 years old. Note that I broke my own rule of doing this before Step 1A: Disability Insurance. It was not an either/or decision, or a case of not following my own advice; I simply had little education on disability at the time and then dragged my feet for a couple of years, as previously mentioned. I also figured if I was going to buy insurance with the little surplus I had, I wanted to at least know I would get something out of it, and Whole Life was the only kind that could guarantee I could get my money back plus interest. My first life insurance policy was a $100,000 Whole Life plan that cost $110 monthly.

I had met with enough wealthy clients to learn from them that taxes were an ever-changing, never-ending nightmare and that successful people seemed to be more concerned with protecting their money than growing it. This fit nicely with the guarantees and tax advantages that Whole Life cash value could offer me. I deferred on Term (or even a blend including Term) because I was single and without kids. But being at least proactive enough to know that when that day came, even if I stayed in great health, it would be more expensive for an older version of me to buy the same thing, I appreciated my new death benefit. My policy also includes a rider that allows me to continue adding coverage throughout my life at a good health rating without ever doing a medical review again, an accelerated benefit feature, and a disability waiver of premium (all features I recommend be on every policy).

Since then, I have added two more Whole Life policies totaling $1 million face amount and a $3 million convertible term policy as I try to stay up to date with my overall financial plan. You'll read soon about how this was never a hindrance to my retirement planning or investment portfolio, but rather a compliment each step of the way. While my annual outlay to equities far exceeds that of life insurance, I continue to view my Whole Life plans as the immovable foundation that I can rely on regardless of interest rates, tax changes, politics, or market ups and downs.

FREQUENTLY ASKED QUESTIONS

Instead of using the Human Life Value (HLV) formula, can I just use a cost coverage ratio?

Answer: A coverage ratio is a financial metric that assesses a company's or individual's ability to meet its financial obligations, particularly those related to debt servicing. Using this approach could work, but it adds much more room for error. If a young household were to assess their current bills and debts (e.g. the mortgage, two auto loans, a student loan) and buy enough life insurance to pay these off in full, that could leave the surviving spouse debt-free, but then what? If this hypothetical couple were to look beyond a static snapshot of today, and foresee future expenses (e.g. kids' college tuition, funding retirement plans for the next 30 years, annual vacations, a home renovation, etc.) the coverage ratio quickly expands. Perhaps the best insight of the last sentence was the "etcetera," the myriad of expected and unexpected bills that occur through everyday living. In summary, a perfect cost coverage ratio should eventually meet the Human Live Value figure, unless the financial plan is based on the widow willingly increasing their workload while decreasing their lifestyle and expenses.

Is life insurance cash value really accessible tax-free?

Answer: It can be. The preferential tax treatment surrounding life insurance has always existed based on its original nature of protecting widows and children. This tax treatment allows the death benefit to be income tax-free, regardless of the size of the policy, and possibly completely tax-free if not subject to estate or inheritance taxes. This favorable status also carries over to the cash value in that it can grow tax-deferred and is accessed on a FIFO basis (First-In, First-Out accounting method). The policy owner can withdraw their basis (the total of the premiums paid) tax-free and/or borrow against this cash-value, which is a nontaxable event. This is a possible efficiency versus taxable savings or investment accounts, whose interest and dividends may be taxable annually and face eventual capital gains taxes. Note: if the policy is deemed a Modified Endowment Contract (MEC), the cash value can be taxed on a LIFO basis (Last-In, First-Out) meaning the gains come out first and are subject to ordinary income tax, additionally they may be subject to a 10 percent early withdrawal penalty for those under the age of 59½.[10, 11]

Is permanent life insurance an investment?

Answer: No. While permanent life insurance policies usually have a cash value, sometimes even tied to the stock market in Indexed Universal Life or Variable Universal Life, it is technically not an investment. However, cash values can be seen as another asset in an individual's portfolio. Participating policies, those that can declare dividends, such as Whole

[10] A Modified Endowment Contract (MEC) is a life insurance policy that fails to meet the federal guidelines called the TAMRA (Technical and Miscellaneous Revenue Act of 1988) "seven-pay test." It may be the result of paying excess premiums in too short a period creating too much cash value. IRS Section 7702.—Life Insurance Contract Defined (Also § 7702A.) Rev. Rul. 2005-6

[11] Clients should consult with their legal and tax advisors to discuss their personal situations.

Life, can offer diversification against stock market risk, bond interest rate risk, and default risk. Index and variable policies are not as effective as a market diversifier due to their index or mutual fund correlations.

Can I change my beneficiaries?

Answer: So long as the beneficiaries are not designated as irrevocable beneficiaries, or held inside of an irrevocable trust, the policy owner generally can update beneficiary designations at their discretion.

Should I name my minor child as a beneficiary?

Answer: Because minors generally cannot manage their own money, some life insurance carriers will require a legal guardian to be named as the beneficiary or designate them under the Uniform Transfers of Minors Act (UTMA). It is often considered best practice to have a minor's trust drafted and named as a beneficiary to properly manage and distribute any death proceeds for the benefit of the minor beneficiary.

What is the contestability period?

Answer: This is the defined time frame in which the insurance company can investigate an application for fraud or misrepresentation and potentially deny a claim, typically two years from the policy's issue date. Many policies have a suicide clause, which allows the company to deny a death claim if the insured dies by suicide within this time frame. An insurer may still be able to deny a claim after the contestability period if they can prove intentional fraud on the application.

PROTECTION FROM CREDITORS AND PREDATORS

Steps 1A and 1B protect you from your own frailties due to illnesses or injuries. Unfortunately, not only is financial planning not done in a laboratory, but it is not done in a vacuum either. There are over 8 billion people in the world today. Sometimes, innocent people accidentally harm others, and sometimes malicious people intentionally harm others.

Another block in the foundation of financial planning is liability insurance. One of the most crippling blows in financial planning comes when it seems like you've done all the right things, established a good career, protected your income and family, worked hard and saved for decades…only to watch an entire balance sheet be ravaged by a court ruling. We live in a litigious society, lawsuits are filed every day all around the world. People can protect themselves from financial damages following an accident via property and casualty insurance. Auto insurance, homeowners insurance, and personal liability umbrella policies all fit into this category.

Liability coverage kicks in whenever the insured is at fault and subject to a lawsuit or paying an injured party. These oft-overlooked line items can be the difference between sheltering one's balance sheet and facing overnight bankruptcy. Why are they overlooked? For many of the same reasons we've already discussed: pretending bad outcomes don't happen or else due to cutting costs (often, an insurance agent's perceived value is graded by how much they can "save" a customer, rather than by how much protection they can provide).

Liability insurance can get lost in the shuffle, with auto and homeowners being connected more with the physical asset. Policyholders who glance at their declaration page may look first to their "collision" limits for auto, making sure the car they love is fully insured. The same goes for "property" limits for protecting their house. A fender bender may be more common than a lawsuit, and receiving $5,000 from the insurance company can get the car back on the road, but owing an injured party hundreds of thousands, sometimes millions of dollars, can do a lot more than take a car off the road.

An umbrella policy can go above and beyond auto and homeowners limits to provide extra coverage. Typically sold in blocks of $1 million, this insurance can cover defense costs, personal injury, libel, slander, rental properties, and more.

Regarding rental properties, one of the most popular forms of asset protection has become the limited liability company (LLC). In short, an LLC is a business structure that provides the limited liability of a corporation with the typically less complex taxation as a pass-through entity, such as a partnership or sole proprietor. It is meant to isolate the finances of the underlying business from the rest of the business owner's world. Landlords can put their properties in LLC's, just as other businesses do, to shelter a claim stemming from a property to the rest of their financial plan. There is much more to learn about asset protection, corporations, and trust-owned assets that goes beyond the content of this book and involves the assistance of legal counsel.

WHAT DID I DO?

I followed the advice of my Property and Casualty agent and purchased the maximum collision and property coverage for my cars and homes, and maximum liability limits ($500,000 through my particular carrier). I opted for a $1,000 deductible, saving some premium versus a $500 deductible, as I considered smaller claims of the $500-$800 variety manageable and not worth jeopardizing future insurance rates by creating a claims history. For those new to insurance lingo, the deductible is the out-of-pocket expense the insured is responsible for before their insurance coverage kicks in. The higher the deductible, the lower the premium, and vice versa.

I also purchased the maximum personal liability umbrella policy allowed, initially $3 million, which I review annually to keep commensurate with my financial situation. Full disclosure, I have received conflicting recommendations from risk mitigation experts about putting my various rental properties each in their own LLC to provide maximum isolation, and other recommendations that suggest having each property listed on the umbrella policy is adequate. I am sure there are good cases to be made for each, but I have continued to own the properties outright and have them covered by a substantial umbrella policy.

FREQUENTLY ASKED QUESTIONS

Are professional liability and personal liability two separate things?
Answer: Yes. A professional policy, such as Errors & Omissions or Malpractice, is meant to cover liability in the workplace. A personal liability policy that includes home, renters, and auto insurance is completely separate.

Does my liability insurance cover my own injuries?
Answer: No. Standard liability insurance is designed to cover the financial responsibilities for injuries or damages you cause to others. Separate coverages, such as Personal Injury Protection (PIP) are meant to cover your own injuries.

Can I save money by dropping my auto and homeowners limits to the minimum and just buy a bigger umbrella policy?
Answer: Nice try, but most umbrella policies will require their own minimum liability limits on underlying policies. Benefits from an umbrella policy typically kick in after the underlying policies have paid their maximum liability limits. An umbrella is an add-on, not a replacement.

LONG-TERM CARE

The best part of retirement planning is that people are living longer than ever. The worst part of retirement planning is that people are living longer than ever. Longevity is the ultimate risk multiplier. Name any risk in retirement planning—taxes, market volatility, inflation, medical bills, they are all amplified with time.

Medicare/Medicaid has become the largest line item on the U.S. budget, costing more than $1.7 trillion annually. That is nearly $150 billion more than Social Security and almost double what is spent on Defense. In 1990, nearly twice as many funds were allocated to both Defense spending and Social Security, versus Medicare and Medicaid.[12]

As mentioned previously, the fact of aging is that you will either die suddenly or you will become 100 percent dependent on someone else for your care. The question is: when total dependency occurs, how long will it last? With advances in 21st-century medicine, this later phase of life has been prolonged. One could argue that quality has been traded for quantity in this stage.

Long-term care includes the services provided to someone who is chronically ill. This is usually someone who needs help performing at least two activities of daily living (ADLs), such as bathing, eating, transferring, getting dressed, or going to the bathroom. According to the Department of Health and Human Services, one in five adults will need long-term care for more than five years, with the average being 3.6 years for women and 2.5 years for men.[13] As of 2024, the monthly median cost of nursing home care in the U.S. is $10,646 for a private room.[14] By the time you read this, that cost will likely be higher, as the increases in the cost of healthcare have routinely exceeded the rate of inflation (Consumer Price Index, CPI).

Medicaid is the primary payer across the nation for long-term care services. Medicaid eligibility varies by state, but in general, it requires the beneficiary to have a very low income and countable assets. Formed in 1965 by President Lyndon B. Johnson, it is a form of welfare meant to protect the health and well-being of low-income Americans in niche circumstances. It was not meant to become the federal government's

[12] U.S. Debt Clock

[13] ASPE Research Brief. "Long-Term Services and Supports for Older Americans: Risks and Financing, 2022" (revised August 2022).

[14] "Cost of Care Survey." Genworth, 2024.

largest expense (I cover the economics of American entitlements in greater detail in *What Should I Do with My Money?*). Recent legislation, such as the One Big Beautiful Bill Act, aims to reduce the Medicaid budget. These reductions primarily target able-bodied working age adults, but there can be a trickle-down effect reducing overall healthcare reimbursements. The pendulum is bound to swing responsibility back towards the individual and away from the government.

The alternative to using Medicaid for long-term care is what is often called "private pay." People who want to age on their own terms with the most freedom of choice can plan to pay their own way. This approach can enable someone to live in a private assisted living or nursing facility, choose their own at-home nurse or aid, and make other decisions that would not be limited or dictated by Medicaid.

Before the advent of long-term care insurance, the only way to achieve "private pay" was by using one's income or assets, essentially self-insuring. However, with the current national median cost of a nursing home mentioned above ($10,646 monthly), a three-year stay could exceed $350,000. For some wealthy seniors, self-insuring may be possible, but it may jeopardize legacy goals or the retirement plans of a surviving spouse.

For people concerned with the costs of long-term care, there are essentially three options to alleviate the burden:

Standalone Long-Term Care Insurance (LTC)

In the year 2000, there were over 100 carriers offering LTC policies. At the time of this writing, there are roughly a dozen selling the product.[15] Premium rates cannot be guaranteed on LTC policies, and almost

[15] "The Collapse of Long-Term Care Insurance," Prospect. Alexander Sammon, 10/20/2020.

all in-force policies have offered their clients the option to either reduce benefits or pay an increased rate. Most major carriers have left the field as claims rates and benefits paid far exceeded underwriting expectations, making the product unprofitable to insurance and reinsurance companies. Aside from lower benefits and higher costs, "indemnity" style policies are all but extinct. These plans said that when the insured became chronically ill, they were entitled to their monthly benefit as cash. Now, most policies offer a "reimbursement" format, in which the insured must produce receipts for care, and the policy will reimburse payments up to their monthly benefit. As one could imagine, producing receipts every month while chronically ill can be a tall order, even with the help of an adult child or power of attorney.

Life Insurance with Long-Term Care Rider

Some life insurance carriers are addressing the growing need by offering accelerated death benefit riders. Most will have a contract privilege stating that if the insured becomes chronically or terminally ill, they can access a portion of their death benefit prematurely. Ordinarily, the policy owner can access their Cash Value while living, but with an accelerated benefit, they can also access some of the "Net Amount at Risk," which is the difference between the Cash Value and the Death Benefit. This advance is usually a lien against the Death Benefit. Some carriers also offer a true Long-Term Care rider that can serve a similar purpose, but often allow a larger portion of the Death Benefit to be accessible without the accruing interest of a policy loan. By owning a permanent life insurance policy, such as Whole Life, the insured may be able to spend down their retirement assets and portfolio more confidently for long-term care costs, knowing that the eventual tax-free death benefit can replenish the bucket. The advancement feature provides just another option to access more cash.

Hybrid Long-Term Care

There are obviously several shortcomings of standalone LTC, as previously alluded to—nonguaranteed increasing premiums, reimbursement benefit issues, financial woes of the carrier, etc. However, one of the hardest pills to swallow for LTC buyers was the fact that they could pay for a policy for 30+ years, die suddenly, and have nothing to show for a significant outlay of premiums. A number of carriers have created a form of life insurance with cash indemnity long-term care benefits that is often paid with one lump-sum deposit. The policy creates an immediate pool of long-term care benefits, which can grow over time, a surrender value, and a death benefit. For people with a large amount of non-qualified assets at their disposal, this policy can address their concerns with the ability to get their premium back if they change their mind in the future or leave a death benefit to heirs in the event that they did die suddenly.

Like all forms of insurance, its purpose is to replace lost income or assets as the result of an unfortunate financial event. The price for all three options can appear high, but its cost may be well worth it if it can provide liquidity and confidence in retirement by mitigating one of the largest risks for senior citizens.

WHAT DID I DO?

Most long-term care planning conversations occur in one's 40s and 50s. After 60, the product may become cost-prohibitive, or it may not be attainable due to medical underwriting issues. Before the age of 40, planning for a long-term care need that is constantly evolving and may be 50+ years away may not be the biggest priority.

I personally own three Whole Life policies. These were originally bought for different reasons based on my station in life at that time, some for the safe, tax-beneficial growth of cash value, and others for a permanent death benefit to protect my family and whatever concerns retirement might bring. While it was not a driver for my purchase at the time, all three contain an Accelerated Death Benefit feature that will be ready for me if needed.

I envision using my portfolio to pay for any long-term care costs that might arise, with the assurance that large tax-free death benefits will more than make up for any subtractions along the way. But if I did need another bucket to access in the future, the Accelerated Death Benefit provision will provide just one more option. As I like to say, I can't predict the future, but I can keep preparing for it.

FREQUENTLY ASKED QUESTIONS

What costs of care are covered?

Answer: Typically, an indemnity benefit only requires the insured to be unable to perform two of six ADLs, and then they are free to use their cash benefit at their discretion. Reimbursement policies may include language as to what types of home health care, assisted living, or nursing home care may or may not be covered.

Do annuities have long-term care?

Answer: Some annuities offer a feature that can increase their income benefit payouts and/or waive any remaining surrender period should the owner be confined to a nursing home or deemed chronically ill.

Are long-term care benefits received tax-free?

Answer: Benefits from tax-qualified long-term care policies may be received income tax-free. Indemnity policies may have a daily limit for tax-free benefits.

ESTATE PLANNING

By now, you may be wondering how so many pieces of paper can be so critical in determining the difference between financial success and ruin. Tis the world we live in. The final element in what I would consider to be the foundation of financial planning (Protection First) brings in our friends from the law department.

Webster's dictionary defines the term "estate planning" as: the arranging for the disposition and management of one's estate at death through the use of wills, trusts, insurance policies, and other devices. This is obviously a broad definition. Technically speaking, when someone buys a life insurance policy, they are estate planning. When someone names a beneficiary on their retirement account, they are estate planning. When Grandpa says he wants his watch collection to go to little Tommy, he is estate planning. This section is best left to the attorneys, but some basics are in order to help the general public make sense of what can easily become legalese.

A will, also known as a last will and testament, is a legal declaration of a person's wishes regarding the disbursement of his or her property. Many couples think they draft one will as a family. They can draft a trust this way, which will be explained momentarily, but wills are done individually.

Here are the key actors in the play, translated from legalese to English:

- **Testator:** The person who creates the will.
- **Executor:** The named person who will be in charge of making sure the wishes outlined in the will are followed.
- **Guardian:** These are the people named who will take care of the testator's children or disabled dependents. Alternate guardians can also be named in case the original guardians are not available.

- **Real Property:** Physical property such as a home or artifacts that the testator owns.
- **Healthcare Proxy*:** Not part of a will, but often done in conjunction, this is a person designated to make medical decisions on one's behalf if they are unable to do so.
- **Living Will*:** Also not part of a will, this document allows one to put in writing medical treatments they would or would not want in the event of becoming terminally ill and incapacitated.
- **Power of Attorney*:** Also not part of a will, this separate document allows another person to make financial, legal, and/or medical decisions for one's benefit while they are alive.

Those definitions with asterisks indicate elements that are often completed with an attorney while drafting a will, but they do not *need* to be. Forms to appoint Healthcare Proxies and/or Living Wills can be provided at a hospital stay for people who have not already completed them.

Baby boomers currently own 52 percent of the nation's entire wealth. Contrast this with millennials, who share an almost equal population size, but own 9 percent of the total wealth in the U.S.[16] As baby boomers begin to enter their 80s and the largest generational transfer of wealth takes place, clear decision making is imperative. If I find a client of advanced age suddenly acting or talking irrationally, continually repeating the same question, or forgetting conversations from just a moment ago, I'll ask if they'd like their most trusted relative to sit in on a meeting (often their adult children or a younger sibling). I also suggest they

[16] https://www.statista.com/statistics/1376622/wealth-distribution-for-the-us-generation/#:~:text=In%20the%20first%20quarter%20of,boomers%20in%20the%20United%20States.

complete a Power of Attorney so that this other individual can help with their financial decisions and paperwork. Like so much in finance, the sooner these decisions are made, the better.

People often mistakenly think that drafting a will governs every asset that they own, superseding anything else previously arranged. This is not true. I have personally seen it shock both those who misunderstood their estate plans but had time to correct them, and times when it was too late, and beneficiaries who expected one thing got completely another. It is critical to understand the difference between probate assets and non-probate assets. Probate assets require court supervision and follow the instructions of the will. People who die without a will, what is called dying intestate, will have their probatable assets disbursed according to state law. Non-probate assets pass directly to designated beneficiaries without the need for court supervision. This often includes life insurance policies, retirement accounts, jointly owned accounts, and other accounts that are Transfer on Death (TOD) or Payable on Death (POD).

Early in my career, I met with an elderly couple who had spent a significant sum on legal fees to draft their wills and other estate planning tools. Their net worth was well over $5 million. However, close to $4 million of this was in Individual Retirement Accounts (IRAs) with named beneficiaries. Additionally, the husband had a large life insurance policy with a designated beneficiary. Upon reviewing their wills, I noted that the goal of their wills was to give their wealth to family members who I noticed were not beneficiaries of either the IRAs or his life insurance policy. When I showed them that most of their money, IRA funds and his life insurance proceeds, would all go to different beneficiaries, they were stunned. "But our wills say this!" he nearly jumped out of his seat. Fortunately, we were able to change the beneficiaries on their IRAs and his life insurance to be in line with the more recent goals of their wills, but this misunderstanding goes unnoticed all too often.

This miscommunication underscores why it is so important for all parties to be on the same page. In the DIY (do-it-yourself) era of completing online templates or learning from YouTube videos, people are more prone to making costly mistakes.

The other major piece of estate planning involves the drafting of trusts. Trusts can be used for tax planning purposes, to limit asset exposure, to further detail the distribution and management of assets, to keep overall estate plans confidential, or any combination thereof. This topic alone could merit its own book and has many times over.

An example of the interplay between assets, corporate structure, and estate planning can be found in the New York Yankees. In 1973, George Steinbrenner and several other minor investors bought the Yankees from CBS for $8.8 million.[17] The Yankees are now worth an estimated $7.9 billion[18] and are managed by George's son, Hal Steinbrenner. Although Hal technically does not own the Yanks—the team is currently owned by Yankees Global Enterprises, LLC, which is owned by a trust set up by George Steinbrenner before his death in 2010. Demanding, impulsive, and outspoken, Steinbrenner earned the nickname "The Boss," yet he and his advisors took the time necessary to safeguard the means to his ends.

It is important for anyone creating or revising their estate plans to recognize that laws are continually changing. Some factors are federal law, and others are governed by state law, all changing with the years. Clients should review their estate plans with their attorneys, CPAs, and CFPs as their financial situation evolves and when tax laws necessitate doing so.

[17] Madden, Bill (2010). *Steinbrenner: The Last Lion of Baseball.* HarperCollins.

[18] https://www.sportico.com/feature/mlb-team-values-rankings-list-1234715821/

WHAT DID I DO?

The portion of my assets that I want to go outright to specific people with "no strings attached," if I were to die, they are free to do whatever they please, are listed as primary beneficiaries on my various accounts and life insurance policies. This is the simplest and quickest way to transfer wealth and give the beneficiary full control and responsibility of said inheritance. I fully recognize this opens unlimited outcomes to this portion of my eventual bequest, from being blown on an antique car collection to being erased by a divorce or unexpected lawsuit, which is why not all of my wealth is to be transferred this way.

When I got married, my wife and I drafted a popular estate tool called a QTIP Trust (Qualified Terminal Interest Property Trust). In short, a QTIP Trust can provide for the surviving spouse while still controlling how assets are distributed once the surviving spouse dies. Income generation from the assets in the trust and a portion of the principal are paid to the surviving spouse. Once the surviving spouse dies, the remaining assets of the QTIP Trust are paid to named beneficiaries, which in our case is a family trust that guides money for future generations. Both trusts have a named trustee, a sibling, who is in control of the asset management of the trusts, distribution of assets, and can allow special distributions in the cases of an ascertainable standard called HEMS (health, education, maintenance, or support).

The textbook practitioner could argue that as soon as one owns assets, be it a house, a life insurance policy, investments, etc., he or she should draft estate plans. In my mid-20s, this would have been financially advisable. However, emotionally, I was not concerned as I truly did not have any dependents at the time, hence my delay. My parents and brother were more than capable of inheriting my money if I died unexpectedly. Once I was married and had a family, the complexities and potential outcomes became as vast as they did meaningful.

Like so many areas of planning, there is the financial component and the emotional component. I understood the financial, but the emotional is usually what pushes one to action. I'll share another story that convinced me to call my attorney.

I had an elderly client who I knew personally very well. She was in her late 70s when her husband passed away and she decided to remarry shortly thereafter. Much of her wealth was from her late husband, to whom she was married to most of her adult life. Upon meeting with her and her new husband, who was nearly 80 years old, I told them both that updating their wills and drafting trusts would be in their best interests to not only protect themselves, but also any planned bequests to their respective children.

The lady immediately replied, "Bryan, I understand, but we both agree that at some point in life, you just have to trust one another."

Despite my recommendation, they named one another 100 percent beneficiary of their assets. One year later, the wife (my original client) passed away, leaving all of her wealth, mostly from her prior husband, to her new husband. While she made her wishes well known to everyone in that her assets were to pass on to her three children, one of whom was disabled, her surviving husband quickly called me to make his children 100 percent beneficiaries of all the money he'd just received. Aside from an honest, "You know that's not what she would have wanted," there was nothing further I could do. In short, three children were effectively disinherited from their biological father's life savings by three other adult children they had never met before.

I know a lot of people will say they don't care what happens once they are no longer here, but that was enough for me to spend an hour with my attorney and put my wishes down on paper.

FREQUENTLY ASKED QUESTIONS

How often should I update my estate plans?

Answer: Any time there is a major life event, such as the birth of a child, marriage, divorce, or death in the family. Besides these triggering events, it is always a good idea to review estate plans every three to five years. I have seen professionals such as CPAs or financial advisors named as trustees in estate plans who have since retired.

Should I tell my executors, trustees, and beneficiaries who they are?
Answer: Usually yes. There may be circumstances when the grantor does not want their children or beneficiaries to know that they will someday inherit possibly significant wealth, for fear of their complacency, or to prevent any jealousy. However, punting the problem to a time when the patriarch or matriarch is no longer here can sometimes compound issues. Being an executor and/or trustee can be a time-consuming task that the appointee may not be up for; it may be wise to discuss your intent with these individuals to make sure they are capable, responsible, and willing. Also, beneficiaries may not want to inherit wealth if they are dealing with their own financial issues, such as a looming divorce or legal trouble.

Are wills public record?
Answer: Yes. While a will is not public record during the testator's lifetime, once they die and it is filed with the probate court it becomes a public record. This is how the estates of Marilyn Monroe, Princess Diana, James Gandolfini, and other celebrities who forwent trusts are so well known. Trusts are generally private documents that do not become public records.

Do trusts pay taxes?
Answer: Sometimes. As of this writing, trusts are taxed at the highest federal income tax bracket, starting at $15,650 of annual trust income.[19] These income tax consequences should not be overlooked when doing estate tax planning, which may not be as necessary when applicable exclusion amounts from federal estate tax are very high.

[19] https://www.fidelity.com/viewpoints/wealth-management/estate-planning-common-pitfalls

The goal of financial planning is efficiency. No one wants to take two steps forward and one step back—or worse yet, one step forward and two steps backward. The next three steps do not care how old you are, how healthy you are, if you skydive for fun or operate on brains for a living, if you have been in four car accidents or none. Step 1 is the only step that becomes less efficient and less practical with each waiting day. That is why protecting your pathways to wealth, and then protecting each asset as it is accumulated, must always be the priority. Remove the worries before they even have a chance to disrupt your plans.

STEP 2

CASH IS KING

"Revenue is vanity, profit is sanity, but cash is king."

—Anonymous

WHETHER MONEY IS in your back pocket, a five-minute drive to the ATM, tied up for the next year in a bond, locked up until age 59½ in your 401(k), or in the form of home equity standing behind a lender with a lengthy underwriting review, all these sources of money have varying degrees of **liquidity.**

Liquidity can be defined as the degree of ease and speed with which you have access to capital. The liquidity value of different assets will be discussed in detail in Step 4, but for now, the point is to realize that there is such a thing as liquidity value. I am often asked, "What is the biggest financial mistake young professionals make?" The answer is: ignoring liquidity.

Liquidity is necessary for two simple reasons: emergencies and opportunities. Any beginner's guide to financial planning will address the value of maintaining an adequate emergency fund. While this is true, there is also a fun way to look at the exercise of saving money, in that cash also creates an opportunity fund.

Even if you find yourself unmotivated by fear, wouldn't you like money ready to go when something exciting comes along? Like waking up to go to the gym, whether your goal is to look good or to not look bad, the motivation does not matter as much as getting the job done.

"Money is meant to be spent. You can't take it to the grave with you."

Life is surely meant to be enjoyed, but striking a balance between the present and the future is the purpose of financial planning. Those with aggressive financial behavior might seek to reinvest every available dollar in their next venture, versus conservative minded individuals who prefer to hoard every dollar in the bank. Regardless of these natural inclinations, every financial situation calls for an optimal level of cash, meaning there can be both too little and too much.

I empathize with people who do not want to accumulate liquidity. It's like staying in on Friday night when all your friends are going out. I call cash a necessary evil. Sure, liquid money could be spent and enjoyed today or invested to grow at a potentially better rate somewhere else, but this assumes we are in total control of our universe. When life throws a curveball, from needing new tires on the car to fixing a leaky sink, there are two options—pay cash and move on, or finance it.

Financing comes at a cost, from the interest owed on a loan and the lost opportunity costs on that money, to the emotional strain of continuing to pay off a problem that occurred long ago. What seems most unfair is that the people needing the most help with such a bill often pay the highest fees. Someone who lacks liquidity is considered a risky borrower to most lenders, and as such, they pay a higher interest rate. This trap of digging further into a hole is a direct symptom of inadequate liquidity.

On the flip side, a "rainy day fund" can become a "sunny day fund." I work with many real estate investors who can easily pay cash for a new property but instead carry mortgages. "Why would you take on debt when you don't need to?" people ask. *That's exactly why I do*, they'll reply.

Liquid customers are ideal customers; as such, they take advantage of their position to get ideal rates and terms to pursue wealth in motion.

They are *helped* by leverage, not hurt by it. They can finance with confidence in knowing that they can make the debt go away when they feel like it. They have options. Successful investors, businesses, and entrepreneurs always have options. Leverage takes place on their terms, not on the unpredictability of the universe. This can seem completely unfair; the person who could absorb higher borrowing costs or a financial shock gets preferential treatment? It's not that it is unfair; it is earned, it is one of the rewards for building liquidity. It is no different than comparing the person who wakes up early, exercises every morning and makes a marathon look like a walk in the park; versus someone who refuses to exercise and makes a walk in the park look like a marathon.

So, what exactly is liquidity? The most liquid asset is **cash.** That is it. Anyone who says otherwise is incurring risk, the risk that there may not be as much money there on the day you need it. Cash is an actual asset class. Cash equivalents can include savings, checking, and money market accounts. In the United States, up to $250,000 per depositor, per insured bank is guaranteed against bank failure by the Federal Deposit Insurance Corporation (FDIC).

A good rule of thumb is to carry at least six months of fixed expenses in cash. Additionally, any specific expenses in the next couple of years should be earmarked as extra cash positions. These guidelines can easily be adjusted for the expected volatility of one's cash flow and financial plan. For instance, a dual-income household in which the husband is a government worker and the wife is a teacher with stable income may negate the household's need to save more than six months' expenses in cash. Whereas a sole-earning household in which the breadwinner has a sales position with variable commission income, may want to hold more cash to offset such volatility.

Even people who are not spendthrifts can accidentally get stuck in a pinch or miss out on limited-time opportunities. Some investors may have great savings habits, as far as how much of their gross income they actually save, but they make errors in where they put their surplus. They are *good* savers, but not *smart* savers. Since cash does not offer much in the way of growth, especially in low-interest rate environments, it is tempting to overlook liquidity value. Such investors may consider cash a losing proposition, always falling short of inflation. In the long-term, there is truth to this assessment; however, the complaint of having too much cash is a complaint, whereas the complaint of not having enough cash often becomes a cry for help. It's like how pilots will look up at the sky on an overcast day and say, "I'd rather be down here wishing I was up there, than up there wishing I was down here."

Why aren't investments considered liquid? Nonqualified investments, meaning those that are not retirement accounts (401[k], IRA, 457, TSP, etc.), college savings plans (529s), or other vehicles that have strings attached based on the account owner's age or specific allowed uses, can offer liquidity on paper. But I often tell clients that if money is invested with a time horizon less than three years, they are not investing so much as they are gambling. In today's day and age of the internet, an investor can liquidate a marketable security such as a stock or Exchange Traded Fund (ETF) and have that money available in their checking account almost instantaneously, making it appear as liquid as cash. However, if the market has a downturn at the time when the investor lacks cash and needs to liquidate those funds, it can force a fire sale. The ease and speed of accessing the invested funds may be acceptable, but if the account's value is 25 percent less than the deposit, there is still a price to pay for mistakenly considering the account liquid.

It is not how your investments perform, but how you perform with your investments. Investors with insufficient cash positions are not fully in control of how they perform with their investments; rather, they are at the mercy of the unpredictability of life and the economy.

People often look at banks as the directors of global finance, profitable institutions that govern the flow of trillions of dollars every day, and wonder how they can operate like the big guys. While it is true that banks are constantly lending and investing money with the goal of earning more money, they are no different than any other household that must be prepared for emergencies and opportunities.

The most devastating financial collapses in history all have one thing in common: a lack of liquidity. The Great Depression in 1929 was a direct result of bank runs; panicked customers ran to their banks asking for their deposits back, which the banks simply did not have on hand. The Great Recession in 2008 had some different factors at play nearly a century later, but the collapse of investment banks like Lehman Brothers and Bear Stearns, or other banks deemed "Too Big to Fail" that went running to the government for bailout funds, felt the same pains of needing cash when they did not have it.

For these reasons, many safety mechanisms have been put into place to prevent such liquidity crunches from causing a contagion across the economy. The Federal Reserve Board requires large banks with consolidated assets over $100 billion to undergo annual stress tests to prove their liquidity. These large banks must keep a minimum Common Equity Tier 1 (CET1) capital ratio requirement of 4.5 percent (this is a bank's highest quality capital that is immediately available), a stress capital buffer (SCB) that varies by bank but must be at least 2.5 percent, plus a capital surcharge of at least 1 percent for global systemically important banks (G-SIBs).[20]

Households would be wise to go through a similar annual stress test to ensure their liquidity is up to par, ready for emergencies and opportunities. In Step 4, I will discuss analyzing assets like a stool with three legs—liquidity, risk, and taxes. So long as money is a means to an end, its liquidity value should be well understood within every plan.

[20] Large Bank Capital Requirements. The Federal Reserve System, August 2024.

ASSET CLASSES RANKED BY LIQUIDITY VALUE

#1. Greenbacks

These are the physical U.S. dollar bills that are becoming less common in our digital age. This is the most liquid asset in the world, readily accepted nearly everywhere, whether it's to pay back a friend for lunch or purchase a new television.

#2. Checking Accounts

A deposit bank account that is available on demand. Cash withdrawals can be made at the bank branch or any ATM. Debit cards can be used like cash at most places of business and digital transfer services like Venmo or Zelle can be attached to these types of accounts.

#3. Savings and Money Market Accounts

Similar to checking accounts but often with a slightly higher interest rate. Depending on the bank or credit union, some of these accounts may limit how many withdrawals can be made every month.

#4. Nonqualified Investment Accounts

These are investment accounts that are not tied to a specific use under the Internal Revenue Code and may be accessed at any time for any reason without penalty. Please note: underlying mutual funds, investments, or annuities may have their own surrender charges or contingent deferred sales charges (CDSCs).

#5. Roth Accounts

These post-tax retirement accounts are intended for retirement and cannot be fully accessed tax and penalty-free until the account owner is at least 59½ years old and the account has been open for at least five years.

However, the account owner's basis (contributions) are accessible tax and penalty-free at all times; only their gains would be subject to income tax and the 10 percent premature distribution penalty for nonqualified distributions. Certain exceptions may apply such as qualified education expenses, first-time home purchases, and death or disability.

#6. 529 College Savings Plans

These are funds which may be used tax and penalty-free for qualified education expenses for the benefit of the named beneficiary. Nonqualified distributions up to the account owner's basis may be accessed tax and penalty-free, but the gains may be subject to income taxes and a 10 percent distribution penalty.

#7. Cash Value Life Insurance

The policy owner's cash value may be accessible tax and penalty-free through withdrawals or policy loans. The age 59½ rule, applicable to qualified retirement plans, does not apply here.

#8. Real Estate

Home equity can be accessed through the sale of the property, second mortgages, home equity loans, or a home equity line of credit (HELOC).

#9. Pretax Qualified Retirement Accounts

These accounts, including 401(k), Traditional IRA, SEP IRA, Thrift Savings Plan, 403(b), and more, generally cannot be accessed penalty-free before age 59½ (though certain exceptions may apply).

#10. Irrevocable Trust Assets

Such assets are subject to the specific terms of the trust and the trustee(s)' powers.

WHAT DID I DO?

I graduated from college and worked as hard as I could for my first paycheck (which took four months to be eligible for in our commission draw system) and immediately began building liquidity. It sounds simple, after all, money is the mode by which every other object is obtained, but it can be hard. The temptations to spend frivolously and have fun all summer after graduation were obvious. But this would complicate larger goals with each step. For instance, I needed a new car—should I finance some of it, or finance all of it? I wanted to move out—rent or own? These things require cash.

As a financial advisor talking about investments every day to prospective clients, it was equally as tempting to invest my limited surplus and jump to Step 4. But I restrained myself, knowing that a small 401(k) that had a good year or bad year would do little to achieve my goals of buying a new car or condo. Fortunately, my income accelerated, and I kept my savings rate in sync with it so that I could afford bigger ticket purchases, with financing on my terms, and without too much fear of a slow month at the office putting me into credit card debt.

Did I invest at all in my early days in the business? Yes, I did open a brokerage account and put some small deposits into it, viewing it more as a "play account" to follow stocks and sectors that I was regularly advising on. I also began contributing 3 percent of my income to my 401(k) once I became eligible for our company match. But these two money moves paled in comparison to my top priority of building my liquid savings.

Since then, I have always maintained at least six months' expenses in my money market account and a buffer of at least double my normal monthly credit card bills in my checking account. There may be situations that warrant having multiple banks, bank accounts, or separate husband and wife accounts, but I generally recommend couples keep one joint savings and one joint checking, which is all I have ever had; anything more often complicates what should be relatively simple.

FREQUENTLY ASKED QUESTIONS

Wait, why is this not Step 1?

Answer: Many people respond to the tips of Step 1 of buying insurance or drafting estate plans by saying, “I can’t afford it. Let me build up my savings first, and then I’ll consider it.” However, there is a saying in insurance that if you can’t afford the premium, you’ll never be able to afford the problem. Just as you open an umbrella before it starts to rain, or a soldier puts on his armor before going into battle, protecting yourself must come first, or else the savings you worked so hard for are in jeopardy of being taken away. Starting from the beginning is never easy, but starting over again is even harder. Also, do not forget that many forms of insurance critical to a sound financial plan (e.g. life and disability insurance) are not guaranteed to always be available; one bad check-up or health scare could eliminate the best options or make them extremely expensive.

What are some tips to become a better saver?

Answer: People are always looking for ways to save a buck, take a shortcut, or find a silver bullet. It is one of the more common media requests that I receive: “Offer us some tips on saving money!”

The reality is that saving is the most basic aspect of financial planning—inflows versus outflows. It’s what makes saving such a timeless topic; there is no easy solution, no matter how badly we all want one. Sure, you can make gradual improvements by eating at home, carpooling, not going out as much, bundling your streaming services, turning out the lights, clipping coupons, and the list goes on.

Ultimately, it comes down to forcing yourself to save more money. This can come through working overtime or finding a second job, or shifting your lifestyle to reduce expenses. I typically recommend setting up a separate account that is out of sight and out of mind, whether it is the savings account or a separate money market account, and setting up automatic contributions or payroll deposits directly to this. This forced savings accomplishes the old adage of "pay yourself first," rather than creating endless budgets to try and pay everyone else and then save whatever might be left.

Accumulating savings is *the* prerequisite—the training camp, if you will—to investing. It allows you to develop good budgeting habits without incurring any risk. Equally as important, adequate savings can be the buffer against the pain felt by so many in our next step: toxic debt.

STEP 3

CONTROL YOUR DEBTS

"Who goeth a borrowing goeth a sorrowing."
—Benjamin Franklin

Ben Franklin's warnings against the dangers of debt, found throughout his *Poor Richard's Almanac*, certainly carry the ring of truth. But the reality is that most of the great things we enjoy today, from homes to cars and business to technological advancement, are all built on the back of almighty **debt.** Without this leverage, ideas remain ideas, small businesses stay small businesses, and emerging markets never emerge. We all need a little help from a friend from time to time, and in the world of finance, debt can be that friend.

Labeling debt a "friend" probably sounds taboo to most people. But like there are best friends, fair friends, and sometimes bad friends, so too does debt come in different forms. When mom and dad say, "Here's some money, just pay us back when you can, no rush," such *debt* feels like our best friend. What usually starts as an interest-free family loan conveniently morphs into a forgivable loan. Hence, financial professionals like to call family loans "gifts." On occasion, these helpful loans occur in the real world, from forgivable small business loans and grants to subsidized school loans.

Then there are fair friends, the banks and lenders of the world who provide capital to individuals and businesses at prime rates (the rate banks charge to their most creditworthy customers) so their customers may obtain that which they so badly want, with both parties agreeing on the interest due to be fair. This middle ground, our fair friends, are what make capitalism thrive, the win-win situations of finance.

Bad friends are the ones who charge egregious rates of interest, most notably credit card companies. But these seemingly unfair interest rates are not without reason. Someone who is either unlikely to repay their debts or uses their leverage to pursue risky endeavors cannot escape the truth of moral hazard.

Moral hazard is the economic term meaning that someone may take excessive risks or act imprudently because they believe that someone else can pick up the costs. This is the risk mom and dad take in granting multiple loans to their children, who become conditioned to not *needing* to repay them. The unfriendly lenders of the world can justify their pound of flesh to offset the risks of going into business with those of poor credit. They may feel absolved in every situation, saying, “If you don’t like our terms, you’re welcome to go somewhere else.”

The middle ground, fair debt, is largest in strong economies. This is the optimal space where lenders don’t *need* to make the loan, and borrowers don’t *need* to accept it. This is where a lender who reaches too high and tells their customer, “If you don’t like our terms, you’re welcome to go somewhere else,” watches their customer confidently walk right out the door.

Once a client has checked off the first two steps of being well protected and liquid, they should understand their debts owed and debts available. When Step 3 commences, the priority is to eliminate any high-interest debts, the “bad friends.” These are debts that charge interest rates significantly higher than prime rates.

Credit cards are most synonymous with this category. As alluded to earlier, such lenders may appear to charge unfair interest rates, drawing comparisons to being strong-armed by the mob, but they exist because the risks of lending to those with poor credit warrant it. In other words, many such loans are never repaid, left to default as the lender writes off uncollected balances as losses. Furthermore, credit cards are a form of "unsecured" debt, meaning there is no asset (e.g. house, car, boat, etc.) securing the loan.

It is important to realize that while revolving debt like credit cards may charge extremely high interest rates, there is nothing mandating that every customer must pay it. A customer who charges their month's expenses and then pays off their balance in full before the due date, then repeats this process every month, can literally pay zero interest for this monthly leverage. Not only that, but they can be rewarded for utilizing leverage through an array of cashback programs. Credit card companies are so aware of the potential profits they can earn on customers who spend more than they can pay off that they compete with one another through rewards programs, teaser rates, and other costly marketing programs to lure customers in who routinely stay one step behind.

The anxiety associated with personal finance is nowhere more apparent than amongst those struggling with credit card debt. Lingering balances are truly poison to a financial plan. I once asked my Brazilian Jiu Jitsu coach how to deal with being stuck in a very deep choke, and he simply replied, "Don't end up there." That is the best advice for handling credit card debt, too, but people can get stuck in these two unfortunate categories.

First, there are those who unexpectedly fell into a tough situation, whether from a bad investment or a young professional who, in survival mode, began accruing credit card debt before Steps 1 and 2 were even possible. As a financial advisor, such clients do not worry me too much. Life is full of ups and downs, and if this financial down is a one-time out-of-character experience, it can be dealt with. It is no different than an excellent athlete who incurs a sprain; it may feel like an unfair, devastating event, but it doesn't change their winning character, and they will be back in the game soon enough.

The second category of those who feel like they are being strangled by credit card debt are the repeat offenders. They have folded this perpetual debt into their financial plan. They are on the proverbial hamster wheel, forever one very costly step behind. In this situation, getting out of the red requires a complete mind shift. If the first category of credit card customers were those coughing from a bout of strep throat, this is the category of those coughing with a cigarette hanging out of their mouth.

Consumers should also be wary of the age-old tactic used by retailers, nicknamed "spaving." This concept of "spend more to save more" has worked for decades on consumers who believe fads and marketing plans are truly there to save them money. Examples of this include everything from buy one get one free, save an extra 10 percent by opening a store credit card today, or free shipping and handling when you spend over $100. There are endless strategies of luring consumers into buying more than they want or need, for fear of missing out (FOMO) on what appears to be a deal. Shoppers would be wise to only buy what they originally intended; then, if it qualifies for a "spaving" discount or bonus, consider themselves lucky, rather than chase such deals that rack up unnecessary credit card balances.

"But I want to start investing. If I can grow my money quickly, then I don't need to worry about these darn credit cards."

It always feels contrary to be the financial advisor discouraging new clients from investing, but this common plea edifies the importance of the four-step process. People who skimp out on Step 1: Protection First risk being robbed of Step 2: Cash is King and end up struggling with Step 3: Control Your Debts as a result, making Step 4: Wealth Maximization futile.

Someone with $10,000 of persistent credit card debt at 20 percent interest will pay $2,000 annually in interest. For them just to break even, forget about getting ahead, they must invest the same dollar amount at an equal guaranteed rate of return. If, hypothetically speaking, the risk-free rate of return (that of a one-year treasury bond) is 4 percent, there is a negative 16 percent spread against the credit card. Even an investor who exceeds the risk-free rate with a 10 percent or 15 percent return is still in the red because of their high-interest rate debt. It's like watching someone who can only run 6 miles per hour on a treadmill set to 10 miles per hour, bound to fall off and get hurt. They would be wise to hit the big red STOP button first, pay off toxic debt, and then get to work.

Persistent high-interest credit card debt has been established as the top priority for Step 3. But what about all the other forms of debt? There should always be a plan to eliminate debt, but in some scenarios, a borrower can consolidate or trade various forms of debt for preferential interest costs.

Let's look at a summary of the order in which debts should be addressed:

#1: CREDIT CARDS

These little pieces of plastic are one of the most widely used forms of payment across the globe. Over 82 percent of American adults own at least one.[21] Banks and financial services companies issue lines of credit to their customers, who can then borrow against them or "charge" them to pay for goods and services. Credit cards may have annual fees and often are subject to the highest interest rates in the lending world. Despite the bad rap, smart credit card usage can be

[21] https://wallethub.com/edu/cc/number-of-credit-cards/25532

helpful in improving a credit score, and it is one of the few debts that, if paid in full on time, may not be subject to any interest at all. Loose spenders would be wise to set self-imposed limits and keep only one, at the most two, credit cards. Conversely, frugal spenders should not hide from credit cards, but build their credit history through smart leverage. Credit cards are just a tool. Like a length of good rope, it can be used to pull yourself up in a temporary pinch…or to hang yourself.

#2: PERSONAL LOANS

These are typically unsecured loans, not all that different from a credit card. An "unsecured" loan means that there is no asset or collateral backing up the loan. This is obviously riskier to a lender in that if the borrower were to default, the lender may be left out to dry without any way to recoup their funds. People with significant credit card balances may pay them off by acquiring one personal loan, a form of debt consolidation, with a better interest rate, but often not that much better than a credit card.

#3: AUTO LOANS

This is the first form of "secured" debt on the list and will typically carry a better interest rate than credit cards or personal loans. If it is secured, then why doesn't it get the best rate? As most car owners can attest, a vehicle is a depreciating asset. The day it's driven off the lot, it is instantly worth significantly less than the sticker price. The cost of interest in auto financing can vary widely based on the buyer's credit score and is often baked into the deal. Many car dealerships are willing to go lower in negotiations if the buyer is looking to finance, as they recoup some of the difference in future interest payments.

#4: LINES OF CREDIT

This type of debt is similar to credit cards in that the borrower may have a credit limit they can go up to, and it does not incur any interest cost until funds are borrowed. It is different, though, in that it is usually a secured debt. These can be business lines of credit backed by business assets or equipment, securities-based lines of credit backed by the borrower's investment portfolio, or cash value lines of credit backed by the borrower's life insurance cash values. The rates can vary based on several factors, from the borrower's credit history to the type of asset securing the line of credit.

#5: WORKPLACE RETIREMENT PLAN LOAN

These types of loans go against an employee's retirement plan at work, whether it be a 401(k), 403(b), Thrift Savings Plan, pension, etc. As of this writing, most plans stipulate that the employee can borrow up to 50 percent of their vested balance up to a maximum of $50,000. Generally, the loan must be repaid within five years from disbursement. If the employee defaults on the loan or separates service while there is still a balance outstanding, the amount unpaid is typically considered a distribution that will be subject to income tax and a 10 percent early withdrawal penalty if the employee is under age 59½. Many workplace retirement plans do not allow the employee to contribute to their plan while actively repaying a loan, which can slow down their retirement savings rate and cause them to possibly miss an employer matching contribution.

#6: STUDENT LOANS

At the time of this writing (2025), this is one of the most controversial forms of debt (see Chapter 2 of *What Should I Do with My Money?*

for a detailed breakdown of the student loan epidemic). It could be considered a hybrid form of secured/unsecured debt. Technically, there is no asset securing the loan, save for a paper diploma assuming the borrower completes their education. However, it is theoretically secured in that the asset is an educated borrower, who upon completion of their schooling is ready to enter the workforce at a higher compensated job than would be attainable otherwise.

There are an array of forgiveness options available to student borrowers, depending on where they work and who they work for. The most notable program is currently the Public Service Loan Forgiveness (PSLF). Some student loans may be subsidized (the lender pays the interest while the student is in school or in deferment) while others are unsubsidized (i.e., interest begins accruing as soon as the loan is disbursed). Since the passing of Trump's One Big Beautiful Bill Act, there will now be a $257,500 lifetime borrowing limit on all federal student loans (granted, borrowers can still pursue more debt through private lenders).

#7: MORTGAGES

This historically is the best form of debt for several reasons. First, it is secured by an asset that is typically appreciating in value, real estate. If someone cannot pay their mortgage and goes into foreclosure, the bank can take comfort in the fact that it can eventually take ownership of the property and sell it to recoup its funds.

Second, with home ownership being one of the staples of the "American Dream," most borrowers will be able to take advantage of certain tax benefits such as mortgage interest deduction or property tax deduction (currently depends on if the borrower itemizes or takes the standard deduction on their tax return and subject to SALT [State and Local Tax] limitations). Third, the loan repayment can be at a guaranteed interest rate, often for long periods of time, such as a 20 or 30-year fixed mortgage.

With all of that said, a mortgage is often an individual's largest debt, and even good debt deserves to be scrutinized. A good rule of thumb is for annual mortgage payments not to exceed 30 percent of gross household income. It is also important Step 2: Cash is King be satisfied first, or new homeowners can find themselves to be "house rich and cash poor," usually a situation rife with troubles. Furthermore, the homeowner should plan to own the financed property for at least 5 years. Mortgage amortization works so that most early mortgage payments go primarily to interest, preventing the buildup of equity for some time.

Since debt involving real estate often carries fair interest rates, it may be advisable for borrowers carrying less favorable debt, like credit cards and personal loans, to trade up to real estate debt. This can sometimes be accomplished through a Home Equity Loan, Home Equity Line of Credit (HELOC), or second mortgage.

These various forms of debt are all affected by the borrower's FICO score, also known as a credit score. FICO stands for Fair Isaac Corporation, the developer of the credit scoring model. A FICO score is a three-digit number that indicates how likely a person is to repay a debt. It is based upon the person's credit history, including payment history, how long they have had credit, how much available credit they have, versus what has been used.

FICO scores typically range from 300-850; the higher the score, the better. Generally, a score below 579 is poor, around 700 is good, and above 800 is exceptional. Most credit reports are tracked by Equifax, Experian, and TransUnion.

"I don't have a credit history. I just graduated and started working, I can't get a loan anywhere. It's not fair."

This situation, which many young professionals or immigrants might encounter, is what is referred to as a "thin file," meaning the individual does not have much credit history. This is not a bad thing, or a good thing, it is a common starting point. A few basic steps to begin building a credit history include applying for a secured credit card. This works just like a normal credit card in that there are limits and interest fees, but it usually requires the borrower to make a security deposit or attach it to a checking account. A fast way to start building credit is to become an authorized user on someone else's card, like a parent or spouse. Once a credit card has been obtained, using it responsibly can help immensely.

Credit cards seemingly present a double-edged sword with this last point. They can become the worst kind of debt with exorbitant variable interest rates if not managed properly, but they also offer one of the best ways to start building a good FICO score. The best approach is to incur manageable debt every month, even just a tank of gas or round of groceries, and then pay the balance in full on time, every time.

WHAT DID I DO?

I am aware that not everyone begins at the same starting line. Some kids work their way through college at minimum wage jobs, enrolling in one class at a time based on whatever they can afford, and finance the difference through student loans that can follow them well into their careers. Other kids start on third base and never have to work a day in their lives, inheriting trust funds before they even know what they want to be when they grow up. The steps outlined above do work for everyone, but where some people may never even have to worry about debt, others may have to work tirelessly to put debt behind them. Anecdotally speaking, I have seen many people struggle with debt early on in their lives, who responsibly control their debts forever thereafter, while many well-off youngsters begin with no debt concerns, only to be controlled by their debts later in life.

As for me, I consider myself very lucky to have fallen in the middle. If there ever seemed to be a financial concern in our family, when my brother or I would ask our parents if everything was ok, they always replied, "We're comfortable." This is certainly a term of relativity, there are people who would have killed for our comfort, whereas others would have thought we were broke.

My starting line included a 4-year college education mixed with scholarships, tuition payments, grants, and federally subsidized student loans. Remember, subsidized loans are the good kind—needs-based loans that do not accrue interest while the borrower is still a student. The inferior option, unsubsidized loans, are not needs-based and begin accruing interest as soon as they are issued, hence why they were a last resort.

I had several friends, some who weren't sure what they wanted to major in and others who didn't take college seriously enough early enough, who ended up pursuing the now-popular 5-year plan. I witnessed how tough this played out for them in that they added to a compounding liability while deferring earning income in the workforce. Other friends of mine went immediately to graduate school, some according to plan to become doctors or attorneys, but others as an unplanned default of not knowing what they wanted to do. This was often worse than the 5-year students, as their balance sheets only became further lopsided in the red.

After graduating from college, I opened a credit card and purchased a certified pre-owned vehicle. I traded in my old Ford Taurus and used my first couple of paychecks as a down payment and financed the balance of my car.

I only had one late credit card payment in my life, which occurred when I overlooked May turning to June while I was at my friend's bachelor party in Las Vegas. I paid off my balance in full on June 2nd, and after calling my bank, I was able to have their $25 late fee waived. This easily could have been reported to any of the credit reporting agencies and caused a ding against my credit score. I don't bring up my record or this one mishap to brag, but simply to underscore how much of a priority it was in that I never took on a credit card balance that I knew could not be fully paid off that month.

The next debt I incurred was my first mortgage on a townhome I purchased when I turned 26 years old, in which I put 20 percent down. I did not entertain buying any property in which I knew I could not put at least 20 percent down and have most of my emergency fund still intact. I had seen enough young clients of mine become house rich, cash poor, and the instant stress that could create. My 20 percent down payment, coupled with paying off what was left of my auto loan and continually eliminating my credit card balances, allowed me to get the best loan terms and interest rate possible, without taking on any private mortgage insurance fee (PMI).

The only other debt I have incurred since this initial stage of my career are mortgages on various investment properties, all of which I put 25 percent cash down as is typical for a conventional mortgage on non-owner-occupied properties. To this point, many clients come to me with the ultimate goal of paying off their mortgage. As I sometimes share my own decisions, they may become perplexed by why I obtain mortgages or maintain them when they could be paid off. This brings back the concept of leverage. Carrying good debt while at the same time being able to pay off said debt can be a great position to be in. This allows me to maintain working capital for other opportunities, invest for potential higher rates of return than those recaptured by paying off a mortgage, and stay liquid on my own terms. In short, it is always advisable to avoid debt when you need it and don't want it, and utilize debt when you want it but don't need it. That is how you control your debts.

FREQUENTLY ASKED QUESTIONS

If high credit card balances are "poison" to a financial plan, why is *this* not Step 1?

Answer: We already established how focusing on liquidity before protection is like building a house with no foundation, but I am sure if you are reading this book and battling credit card debt that feels like a noose tightening around your neck, eliminating debt may feel like the only step that matters. Logically, this makes perfect sense. However, unwanted debt is almost always a symptom of not following Steps 1 and 2. If any of the risks outlined in Step 1 (i.e., lawsuit, disability, premature death, etc.) occur without a contingency plan in place, financial pain follows, with debt often being the only way out. If Step 2 is overlooked (i.e. no emergency fund) and an unexpected bill arises, then debt is the only solution. It may sound counterintuitive to let a bad thing go unchecked, but skipping the first two priorities and throwing all resources at an unwanted debt is like frantically scooping water out of a sinking rowboat as more holes in the bottom crack open. Plug the leaks first and *then* dry it out.

Should I pay off my smallest debts first, just to get them out of the way?

Answer: I know many people want to knock out the little debts first. I get it; it feels good, like checking off an item on the to-do list. However, if you take emotion out of the equation and focus on raw math, it is best to prioritize all resources on the highest interest debts, as these cost the most.

Can I ever ask my creditors for some relief?

Answer: Yes. Most creditors realize that getting some money back from a delinquent customer is better than getting no money back. Your creditors may have debt relief options and payment modifications to help you through a hardship, but you need to contact them and explain your situation.

When should I declare bankruptcy?

Answer: This is the absolute last resort and the option with the longest-lasting consequences. In a Chapter 7 bankruptcy (liquidation), the trustee gathers and sells the debtor's nonexempt assets and uses the proceeds of such assets to pay holders of claims (creditors) in accordance with the provisions of the Bankruptcy Code. The Bankruptcy Code will allow the debtor to keep certain "exempt" property, but a trustee will still liquidate the debtor's remaining assets. This may be a quicker and simpler option to eliminate debt, but it may also involve losing assets. This differs from declaring under Chapter 13 (reorganization), in which the debtor can seek an adjustment or reduction of debts, extended time for repayments, and other reorganization. However, this process can last over 3–5 years and requires consistent income and adherence. (Individuals may be able to save their home from foreclosure in Chapter 13 by allowing them to "catch up" on past due payments.[22])

In a perfect world, there would be unlimited forms of debt with no borrowing limit, zero percent interest, and flexible repayment terms left completely up to the borrower. But as so many movies have popularized, any utopia can quickly turn into dystopia. We live in an economic world based on incentives and disincentives, one in which borrower and lender both have a voice. It is up to you to control debt, to make it a friend not a foe. Only then can you graduate to the fourth and final step of wealth maximization with the wind at your back and the sun on your face.

[22] https://www.uscourts.gov/court-programs/bankruptcy/bankruptcy-basics/chapter-7-bankruptcy-basics

STEP 4

WEALTH MAXIMIZATION

"Rich people work really hard and make a lot of money. Wealthy people work really hard, and their money makes a lot of money."

—Bryan Kuderna

It feels painfully tacky quoting myself to open a chapter, but I say this so often at seminars, and people tell me it's what they remember most. If these were true definitions of rich and wealthy, who wouldn't want to be wealthy?

Every resource surrounding financial planning refers to the pinnacle achievement of financial freedom. It is that moment in life when worry, anxiety, stress, and all their synonyms no longer apply to money. Financial freedom happens when a person reviews their goals and concerns for what they are and not what they cost. This concept of financial independence may sound like a farce, as no one completely ignores cost/benefit analysis. This may be true, so consider financial freedom the time when money is at least not the influencing factor.

Anyone who listens to my podcast or has read *What Should I Do with My Money?* knows that I define wealth according to its Old English etymology: a state of well-being. Everything is relative. Some goals and concerns may cost a fortune, whereas others may not; think a steak and lobster dinner in the city versus a peanut butter and jelly sandwich in the park. Everyone's state of well-being looks different.

The destination may look different from person to person, but the process should not. The process is one built upon help. Without financial help, the best one can do is reach my definition of rich, which is working really hard, a never-ending exercise of labor and frugality, in which the best one can do is get up and do it again tomorrow. The wealthy, on the other hand, value a helping hand. Wealth is a team sport made up of unlimited players, in which you are the owner, general manager, and head coach.

So, how does someone put Step 4 into practice? First, they make sure Steps 1–3 are perfect. If just one part of one of those steps is not up to snuff, then there will exist a gap, an exposure. Such a gap defeats the purpose of the pursuit of wealth by preventing a complete state of well-being. For those aware of their gaps, they can worry forever, hoping disaster avoids them, knowing they are not the only ones in control of their financial plan. For those unaware of their gaps, a disaster can be a blindside hit against a perfect portfolio. Before implementing Step 4 and thinking about risk tolerance, there must be a realistic assessment of risk capacity. The better one has performed in their first three steps, the more risk capacity they will have.

As I introduce the various methods of investing for wealth creation, I will repeat that **an emotional investor is a bad investor**. They are irrational; their gains are lucky byproducts, and their losses are likely results. Conversely, someone who is well-protected, liquid, and free of bad debt can theoretically invest for an unlimited time horizon solely pursuing gain. They are rational.

As we'll discuss in a moment, the process of wealth maximization is built upon smart and efficient compounding. Compounding is the magical helping hand of the wealthy. To illustrate its awesome power, let's explore the greatest real estate deal in history... In 1626, the Dutch led by Peter Minuit bought the island of Manhattan from the Lenape Indians for $24. It is often regarded as one of the most lopsided deals in history, the Dutch having blatantly taken advantage of the natives who lived there.

However, the **Rule of 72**, which calculates how long it will take an investment to double in value by dividing 72 by its interest rate, shows that if the Lenape people invested their $24 at a moderate 7.2 percent annual rate of return, that there $24 would have doubled to $48 in just 10 years by 1636. At the same rate, by the year 1700 their money would be worth $4,100, by 1800- $4.27 million, 1900- $4.32 billion, 2000- $4.7 trillion, and in 2025- $24.7 trillion. So, despite the skyscrapers, ports, Broadway, and Madison Square Garden, Manhattan's GDP which is currently just under $1 trillion, pales in comparison to what the Lenape's $24 could have grown to at 7.2 percent since 1626. Here are some habits to take advantage of compounding and maximize your wealth.

HOW MUCH TO INVEST

The first phase of the last step is building a simple habit: **aim to save 20 percent of your gross income.** This is the food pyramid and workout regimen of wealth management. It's simple to understand, but not always easy to put into practice. If an investor makes $100k annually, they should save $20,000; if they make $200k annually, then $40,000, etc. One reason why the average American household struggles so much with hitting this annual goal is that saving is invisible. It goes unseen. Where is the fun in adding another zero to a bank account statement or 401(k) balance when you can drive a new car, fly first class, or buy a hot tub? The good news is that these ends are not mutually exclusive—you can have your cake and eat it, too. It is just that you should have your cake first, and then eat it, in that order—save, *then* spend.

Notice this advice is based on gross income, the sum of all wages and bonuses *before* taxes and withholdings. Some followers of mine cling to the 20 percent rule but then apply it to their monthly take-home pay or another reduced figure. I applaud the habit, but the investor is only short-changing themselves. They opt to run one kilometer each day instead of one mile.

This instruction is often met with two responses. First, "There's no way I can do that." For many people, that may be true. Perhaps there is credit card debt still hogging up much of the budget, or they are a young family navigating a deluge of bills. They should not be deterred, as it is ok to embrace a goal before it becomes a habit. Only being able to exercise four days a week does not mean completely abandoning the five-day training regimen. As they navigate Steps 1–3, maybe they commit to habitually saving 5 percent of their gross income, then next year it's 10 percent, then 15 percent, and so on. There is no perfect time to start exercising, yet going for a run two days a week is infinitely better than not running at all.

In my opinion, the best way to reach these savings goals is through automation. I recommend every investing client of mine to set up periodic investment plans. This reinforces the habit and removes human error. I find the shorter the mode, the better. Saving 20 percent of gross income in one annual deposit can be a huge lift, dividing it by four through quarterly contributions could be easier, monthly more so, even biweekly or weekly if preferred.

WHERE TO INVEST

The second response I hear is simply, "Where?" Clients of mine are often baffled when my reply to this is, "I don't care." I obviously *do* care, and that discussion will come in due time, but my response is meant to emphasize how superior the 20 percent gross savings habit is to any minutiae within investing. Any personal trainer would choose the person who works out 60 minutes a day without a concrete plan over the person who studies the latest exercise science but can't find their way to the gym. The habit is the foundation, and the "where" is the supplements.

The rest of this chapter will assume that you've fully completed Steps 1–3. If you have not yet built up six months' expenses in an emergency fund as described in Step 2, then most of your 20 percent savings should go to cash. While I often call cash a necessary evil, a buffer for opportunities or unforeseen events with little to no return, it *is* an asset class. There have been down years, such as 2018, in which cash was the best-performing of the major asset classes.

Thereafter, the "where" question for this 20 percent savings should be based first on an investor's time horizon. I constantly tell people that if they do not intend to invest for at least three years, then they are gambling more than investing. Markets fluctuate, even fixed income markets, as interest rates rise and fall or debtors default. As such, the shorter the investment time horizon, the less opportunity the investment has to appreciate or rebound.

A basic way to analyze investment opportunities is like looking at a stool with three legs. In investing, these legs are liquidity, taxability, and risk. Liquidity should be the first consideration, as money's greatest utility is when it can be used. Liquidity and taxability often go hand in hand.

Taxable Accounts

Assuming that cash and cash equivalents occupy the short-term portfolio (zero to three-year range), the next tranche of three-plus years can be considered mid-term. For most investors, these assets fall into taxable accounts. Some examples of taxable accounts include joint, individual, or transfer-on-death (TOD). Notice these are not qualified retirement accounts, college savings plans, or other restricted plans. The primary liquidity concern around taxable accounts revolves around their tax consequence. If an asset is held for more than 12 months before being sold, any gains can receive the preferential tax treatment of long-term capital gains. Conversely, if an investment is held for less than 12 months before being sold, its gains are taxed as short-term gains, which are added to ordinary income.

In addition to the tax consequences of short and long-term gains within taxable accounts, some mutual funds and annuities can have contingent deferred sales charges (CDSC). For mutual funds, most C-shares charge a 1 percent penalty if they are sold within one year, whereas A-shares usually have a larger upfront load but no CDSC, making them ideal for at least a three-year holding period. Institutional and no-load funds may not have any CDSC. CDs do not have a CDSC, but they can have similar early withdrawal penalties if accessed before maturity. Exchange-traded funds (ETFs) and stocks typically do not have a CDSC, making them more liquid.

Taxable accounts do not have any contribution or withdrawal limits, allowing brokerage accounts to have a nearly unlimited balance for higher net worth individuals. It is worth noting that most firms have Securities Investor Protection Corporation (SIPC) protection up to $500,000 if the brokerage firm fails. SIPC is in place to protect customers if their brokerage firm collapses. It is similar to the Federal Deposit Insurance Corporation (FDIC) protection of $250,000 per depositor at FDIC-insured banks to protect against bank collapse. Never make the mistake of thinking SIPC protects you from market loss on your underlying investments.

Tax-Deferred Accounts

The next step in the liquidity ladder is tax-deferred accounts. For most investors, these are long-term investments. Examples of tax-deferred accounts include 401(k), 403(b), Thrift Savings Plan (TSP), Simplified Employment Pension Individual Retirement Account (SEP-IRA),

Savings Incentive Match Plan for Employees (SIMPLE IRA), among others. These are workplace retirement defined-contribution plans that can be funded directly through payroll deductions and possibly employer matching contributions. The different names have to do with IRS tax codes pertaining to the type of employer, such as 401(k) being common among for-profit employers and 403(b) found in tax-exempt organizations like public schools or hospitals.

All of these offer the ability for tax deductions and tax deferral, but their contributions may be different. For instance, in 2025, the maximum 401(k) or 403(b) employee contribution is $23,500 plus an additional catch-up contribution of $7,500 for workers between the ages of 50-59 or $11,250 for ages 60-63. A self-employed person with a SEP IRA could contribute up to 25 percent of their compensation up to $70,000. These figures can change as they are regularly indexed for inflation year by year.[23] The key thing to note is which plan you are eligible for.

Employer matches are an integral part of qualified retirement savings plans and a strong incentive for workers to participate. Since most employers have moved away from costly defined benefit pension plans to defined contribution plans, an employer match has been the tradeoff for many. A common matching formula might say that an eligible employee can receive a 100 percent match up to 3 percent of their income. For example, the worker makes $100,000 and contributes 3 percent or $3,000 to their 401(k), then their employer makes a $3,000 contribution to their plan as well. Many employers now offer a retirement contribution match for employees who pay their student loans (i.e. the priority may be putting 3 percent of salary towards student loans, and the employer matches this payment into their retirement plan). This match can be a very valuable perk when

[23] Internal Revenue Service

saving for retirement. Retirement savers often call the plan's match "free money."

While it is a great incentive, most employer matching formulas include a vesting schedule that requires the employee to work a certain period of time (often three years) before being vested, entitled to the employer portion of the balance. For this reason, someone who thinks they may not last long at their current company should not be contributing solely to catch an employer match, as it may be taken back when they separate service. All these particulars should be able to be answered by a company's human resources (HR) department, the company's group benefits booklet, or the retirement plan's summary description document.

A Traditional Individual Retirement Account (IRA) is another tax-deferred example, but not tied to work. When employees separate service, whether by changing jobs or retiring, it is common for them to roll over their retirement plan assets into an IRA. A qualified rollover continues the tax-deferral, while often offering the plan participant many more investment options.

Annuities are another financial vehicle that provides tax deferral, whether held inside of an IRA or purchased as a nonqualified annuity. Annuities can have surrender periods ranging from a few years to 10 years and beyond, in which the owner would pay a penalty if funds are withdrawn during this time.

The *potential* benefit for retirement plan contributions is in the current year tax deduction allowed for contributions and the corresponding tax deferral. Pre-tax contributions to any of the above plans can provide the taxpayer with a dollar-for-dollar deduction against their current year income. For example, the worker makes $100k and puts 10 percent into their 401(k), reducing their taxable income to $90k. It is critical to realize this is not a tax savings, but rather a tax postponement with a compounding unknown future tax liability. The worker has elected to skip paying taxes on the "seeds" and pay later on the "harvest."

Retirement planning pamphlets like to show a popular, but overly simplified, projection that illustrates the benefits of tax deferral. It goes something like this… A worker making $100k annually could invest $5,000 a year of after-tax earnings throughout their career at an "X" rate of return and retire with a "Y" balance. Or, the same worker could invest $7,000 a year pre-tax inside their retirement plan (reducing their taxable income to $93,000) and, after some hypothetical tax rate, net the same take-home income as the first investor. After the same length of career and assuming the same "X" rate of return, the pre-tax retirement saver has a much larger account balance than "Y" thanks to their larger contributions and years of tax-deferred growth. It almost sounds too good to be true: the retirement plan participant enjoyed the same take-home income and budget in their working years, picked the same investments, and then retired with a much larger balance on their investment statement.

This illustration assumes that all accounts are created equal, that $1 million on one statement is worth the same as $1 million on another statement. This story overlooks or downplays one enormous characteristic, in that every dollar of a pre-tax retirement account will eventually be taxed as ordinary income. The proponent will argue that once the worker is retired, they are automatically in a lower tax bracket or have no income, so what's it matter? Again, a simplified rationale. The retiree may have social security income, pension income, part-time work, investment income, and ultimately ordinary income from their retirement savings distributions. Furthermore, what will tax rates be in 10 years, 20 years, or 40 years?

Shifting from tax consequences back to liquidity concerns, the reason why tax-deferred accounts usually occupy the long-term portion of an investor's portfolio is that they are age 59½ sensitive. This means that withdrawals from a 401(k), 403(b), or IRA before the age of 59½ can be considered premature distributions, subject to penalty. Such distributions would be added to the year's taxable income and would receive an additional 10 percent tax penalty. Some workplace retirement plans may allow a retired worker to access their funds after age 55 if they have separated service but left the plan intact. Workplace retirement plans may offer hardship withdrawal provisions for premature distributions, similar to the exceptions IRAs allow for certain instances up to a limit (such as in the event of a disability or for first-time homebuyers). Workplace retirement plans may also allow loans up to a limit. Traditional IRAs do not allow for loans.

Even with these various emergency access opportunities, retirement plans should always be viewed as for retirement. For investors near 59½ years of age or older, retirement plans can naturally become mid or short-term assets, although their liquidity may still be inhibited at this phase of life as they attempt to withdraw certain amounts year by year to limit tax liabilities.

Tax-Free Accounts

These are types of accounts, or assets in certain instances, which grow tax-free. Some common examples are Roth accounts, whether Roth IRA, Roth 401(k), Roth 403(b), etc., 529 college savings plan, health savings account (HSA), or cash value life insurance. Most tax-free vehicles are built on post-tax contributions, that is, earnings or savings which have already been taxed, providing a short-term pain for long-term gain type of scenario. In retirement planning, Uncle Sam says, "Pay me now or pay me later." These are options to pay the toll now. Because of this structure, such accounts can offer a hybrid of liquidity.

What does a hybrid of liquidity mean? It means that while Roth accounts are qualified retirement accounts, and 529 college savings plans are qualified education accounts, possessing IRS-mandated penalties and taxes against premature distributions, the IRS strings are not *completely* attached. The basis, or contributions, within any of these plans are always available tax and penalty-free. It is the earnings that would be subject to penalty and taxes if withdrawn prematurely. For the Roth IRA, the plan participant would have to be over age 59½ and have owned the account for over five years in order for all of the funds to be accessed tax and penalty-free.

Some people hear this caveat and excitedly commit more funds than originally planned into such accounts, feeling they can get the best of both worlds in tax-free growth without fully forfeiting the liquidity normally surrounding qualified investments. While it may be easier to withdraw some basis from Roth accounts or a 529 college savings plan tax and penalty-free as opposed to a pre-tax retirement plan, in my opinion, the best plans are used the way they are meant to be used. As a financial advisor, I have personally seen far too many investors knowingly contribute short-term funds to Roth retirement accounts and quickly withdraw those contributions for normal budgeting issues. This behavior is not long-term investing and defeats the purpose of building tax-free growth, not to mention that if it becomes too commonplace and the saver must begin withdrawing their gains, it could trigger taxes and premature distribution penalties.

Fans of Roth accounts are probably most familiar with the Roth IRA, which was created in 1997 under the Taxpayer Relief Act of 1997 sponsored by Senator William Roth of Delaware. It was not until 2001, under the Economic Growth and Tax Reconciliation Act of 2001, and in 2006, under the Pension Protection Act, that Roth contributions to workplace retirement plans were made permanently available. The Roth IRA comes with income restrictions that limit how much, if any, funds can be contributed based on the taxpayer's income. In 2025, Single tax filers are completely phased out with modified adjusted gross incomes over $165,000, and for those Married Filing Jointly making over $246,000. These limits are routinely indexed for inflation as well. People often confuse these income limits with all Roth accounts; they only apply to Roth IRAs, and there are currently no income restrictions on Roth contributions to workplace retirement plans.

Retirement savers who do not have a plan through work, or have already maxed out their plan, may turn to the Roth IRA and find themselves blocked by the income limitations. Enter the "Backdoor Roth IRA." This strategy was invented in 2010 when the Tax Increase and Prevention Reconciliation Act lifted income restrictions on converting Traditional IRAs to Roth IRAs. In short, the investor makes a nondeductible contribution to a Traditional IRA and then converts it to a Roth IRA, voila!

529 college savings plans are obviously different from Roth accounts in that they are intended for education-related expenses, but they are comparable in that they offer the ability for tax-free growth. In recent years, their utility has broadened significantly, alleviating many investor liquidity concerns. The 2017 Tax Cuts and Jobs Act expanded the Qualified Tuition Program (QTP) rules to allow up to $10,000 annually of 529 plan funds to be used for primary and secondary education (K-12) without penalty.

Furthermore, the SECURE Act 2.0 of 2022 enabled 529 college savings plan owners to roll over funds to a Roth IRA without federal taxes. The 529 account must have been open and in the beneficiary's name for at least 15 years, the amount being rolled over must have been in the 529 for at least five years, and the beneficiary must have an earned income equal to at least the amount being rolled over. Rollovers are limited to the annual IRA contribution limit, up to a lifetime maximum of $35,000.

The Health Savings Account (HSA) was established in 2003 under the Medicare Prescription Drug Improvement and Modernization Act. It is unique in that participants can get a tax deduction on their contributions, tax-free growth, and tax-free distributions if used for qualified medical expenses. As of this writing, it is the only type of account that offers potentially tax-deductible contributions, tax-free growth, and tax-free distributions.

Investors should by now realize that any of these qualified plans, meaning those driven by specific requirements set by the Internal Revenue Services (IRS), are subject to change. Fortunately, most of these changes have been in the public's favor (i.e. increased contribution limits, increased income limits, added flexibility to premature distributions or plan rollovers, creation of Roth and HSA options, etc.), however, that's not to say congress won't change the rules the other way at some point in the future. Retirement and college savers should note that when there is a tax deduction, tax deferral, or tax-free benefit, there are rules and restrictions present.

Cash value life insurance was alluded to at the outset of this section. Life insurance, in particular Whole Life Insurance, has been used for a long time to provide tax benefits, especially for high-net-worth individuals. As mentioned in Step 1: Protection First, life insurance death benefits can be passed on income tax-free, no matter what the owner's income or net worth is. Death proceeds can be completely tax-free if the policy owner is not subject to estate/inheritance taxes. It is common to hear complaints such as, "The rich get richer," or "How do rich families stay so rich and not have to pay taxes?" While these generalizations are not entirely true, it is true that planning involving permanent life insurance can enable the transfer of large sums of wealth free from taxation.

As it pertains to lifetime value and wealth accumulation, the policy's cash value is made up of post-tax premium payments, which can then grow tax-deferred and be accessed tax-free if the policy is not a Modified Endowment Contract (MEC). The tax-free access can be achieved by withdrawing the policy's premium basis and/or loaning against the cash value. Life insurance cash value can be taxed according to the accounting method of First In First Out (FIFO), allowing the policy owner to access basis before gains. Policy loans against the cash value that are still present at the insured's death, which are in excess of the basis, can be paid off by a tax-free death benefit. In regard to liquidity, this is the one vehicle that is not subject to premature distribution penalties or limitations based on age.

A further explanation of the MEC rules can illuminate the potential value of life insurance. In 1988, the Technical and Miscellaneous Revenue Act (TAMRA) created the term Modified Endowment Contract (MEC). It became necessary as a way to prevent people from using life insurance policies as a tax shelter by overfunding them with large premiums, primarily turning the policy into an investment vehicle instead of a death benefit for families. This practice was considered a tax avoidance strategy, which led to the creation of the "seven-pay test" to identify such policies as a MEC. In short, the same wealth accumulation strategy with preferential tax treatment still exists within the life insurance marketplace, just not quite to the same extent as was available pre-TAMRA.

Taking advantage of tax-free vehicles is akin to swallowing your medicine today rather than kicking the tax can down the road. It can provide more certainty in retirement and allow for tax arbitrage (the practice of profiting from the various ways income and investments are taxed). This is a popular concern for those fearing rising tax rates or higher net worth or income later in life. It can also provide the added benefit of hybrid liquidity not ordinarily found in pre-tax retirement plans.

WHAT TO INVEST IN

Notice we have not even discussed investment opportunities yet, just the buckets they fall within. This delineation between account types and underlying investments is vital. I have been asked more times than I can remember, often by wealthy and educated individuals, which has a better rate of return: the Roth IRA, 401(k), or non-qualified brokerage account? This is like asking which tastes better: a dish, bowl, or mug? The account itself is simply meant to hold investments, or ingredients to stick with the analogy, the actual investments determine the risk/return equation.

Going back to the three-legged stool comparison of liquidity, taxability, and risk, the first step for investors should be to understand the rules of their accounts before exploring their particular investment options. A share of Apple is a share of Apple; it is trading at whatever today's market price determines, its risk/return status is what it is. However, a share of Apple inside of a pre-tax IRA, Roth IRA, or taxable brokerage account can have vastly different liquidity value and tax consequences.

With an understanding of account types in mind, and with the disciplined habit of a target savings rate of 20 percent of gross income, the investor can begin investing. Now, you can ask where, what, and when.

Answering Where to Invest

The answer to *where* should primarily be based upon liquidity concerns. A good investment that needs to be withdrawn in five years turns into a bad investment if it can't be accessed for another 20 years without penalty. The next *where* concern involves tax planning. A good investment that gets taxed at a far higher rate decades from now than originally expected may not seem so good; just as a good investment generating 1099s every year, littered with capital gains, taxable interest, and dividends, may appear to be stumbling along the way. The answer to where to invest is a decision-making process based on account types. Hence, there is no silver-bullet account that everyone ought to be taking advantage of. Most sophisticated investors will have a variety of account types within their financial plan that provide a balance of tax and liquidity pros and cons.

Answering When to Invest

The answer to *when* has plagued investors since the creation of the stock market. Every quoted rate of return simply measures a snapshot in time. This basic fact explains why two investors with the same portfolio can have vastly different experiences based on their entry and exit points. Novice investors who begin during a bull market (rising stock prices) naturally feel optimistic and positive about the concept of investing, with the danger of hubris lurking. Similar investors who begin during a bear market (falling stock prices) are prone to anxiety and possibly cashing out at a loss, with reservations about investing again. Neither necessarily did anything right or wrong; their experience was simply a symptom of timing.

The ebbs and flows of the stock market are great at luring investors into trying to time the market. Mankind has always sought patterns in life, as predictability is synonymous with comfort. For this reason, investors like to identify perceived patterns in the markets and attempt to capitalize on them. No one, I repeat no one, has effectively timed the stock market over an extended period of time. As the famous economist John Maynard Keynes once said, "The market can stay irrational longer than you can stay solvent." The markets do not need to make sense. If you haven't read it already at other points in this book, you're bound to find the famous compliance investment disclaimer that, "Past returns do not guarantee future results. Investing involves risk." For people who feel money must offer a pattern, look no further than a roulette table that has come up red the past 10 spins and the gambler feels black must be due. Believe it or not, the odds of red coming up again are the same as they always are. These mistakes of omission (missing opportunities) and compulsion (acting on false opportunities) are symptoms of not following a process, and likely what caused the Lenape people to lose their $24 fortune.

Questioning *when* to invest, is one more reason why I condone systematic investing. Not only does it take the guesswork out of how to reach a 20 percent savings goal, like going to the gym at 6:00am every day, it also removes the temptation of market timing. Lastly, systematic investing has the added benefit of dollar-cost averaging (DCA). Dollar-cost averaging is the practice of investing a fixed dollar amount on a consistent basis. It can potentially lower your average cost per share of an investment. For example, an investor who invests $100 into Stock "X" every month will buy 50 shares when "X" trades at $2 and 25 shares when it costs $4. They are buying more shares when it is cheaper and fewer shares when it is more expensive. Modal investing should be at a set amount at a set date; the mode can be based upon the investor's budget or preference, but I find monthly contributions to be most effective.

With the *where* (account types) and *when* (monthly, biweekly, etc.) in order, an investor can create a multi-pronged portfolio on autopilot that meets their liquidity and tax planning concerns. This leads to the final question, and the one that receives the most attention: *what* to invest in?

Answering What to Invest In

One of the most widely agreed upon determining factors of *what* to invest in is time horizon. Typically speaking, the shorter the time horizon, the lower the risk tolerance. The period of time the investor participates in during a one or two-year horizon may be positive or negative, but it will not possess the upward trend experienced over a longer timeframe. To avoid having to sell at a loss during a down market, a short-term investor's best course of action is to avoid the risk of a down market through conservative investments or cash equivalents.

Once an investor stretches out their horizon to five to 10 years and beyond, they can start to let their natural risk tendencies take control, as they have now embraced a higher risk capacity. Aside from trading on insider information, ethical investors are subject to the high-risk/high-reward and low-risk/low-reward elements of an efficient and transparent market. Here is where investors need to have a very honest self-diagnosis. Many risk tolerance questionnaires grade an investor's risk/reward appetite with questions like, "Would you be willing to accept an investment that could grow 20 percent but lose 20 percent? Or grow 50 percent but lose 50 percent?"

Answering this question requires a new investor to use their imagination, to think about how they might feel in a scenario that they may never have felt before. I have found many investors to exaggerate their risk tolerance in either direction. Some investors classify themselves as aggressive and seeking superior returns, but then, in a down market, feel anxiety and contemplate selling at a loss. Whereas beginner investors who feel conservative and averse to loss may struggle watching a bull market go by that they wish they were a part of.

I often tell clients that it is perfectly ok to be conservative or aggressive, but to be who you are. If you are conservative, be conservative in up markets and down markets. If you are aggressive, stay aggressive. When investors become emotional investors, transitioning from rational to irrational, jockeying from the conservative to the aggressive and back again, this can be most dangerous. This is emotionally driven market timing.

For long-term investors who are new to financial planning and having trouble identifying as conservative, moderate, or aggressive, they should realize that not every account needs to follow one ideology. Assuming the investor has adequate funds and liquidity, they might consider opening two investment accounts instead of one, letting one be conservative and the other aggressive. You might be asking yourself, "What's the difference? It sounds like window dressing!" In the aggregate, this is true, but the organization might allow the investor to understand first-hand their reaction to market volatility with the comfort that one account addresses a falling market while the other capitalizes on a rising market.

In the 21st century, with smart phones that can show investors every one of their holdings and how they are performing minute by minute with alarming red and exciting green returns, all backed up by blogs, 24/7 business tv shows, and social media posts bragging about the latest winners, the temptation has never been stronger for investors to tinker with their plans. It's best to simply stay the course and tune out the noise. Like a parent who monitors their teenager's screentime, perhaps allow yourself to look at your portfolio only at the end of the week, or just through monthly statements.

The rise of online brokerages that can offer little to no fees without account minimums has empowered almost anyone to be an "investor." While this sounds altruistic at face value, allowing everyone to participate in the potential wealth creation of the markets, it has also created side-by-side apps of online gambling and investing that can be easily blurred. The attraction to high-frequency trading runs counter to the idea that the stock market has long been a place where patience is rewarded, such overactivity is often punished.

Here lies the risk when people say they want to invest, but they don't want a financial plan. A good financial plan does not need to be exciting; frankly, it can be downright boring. It is at odds with the excitement surrounding the markets that is broadcast every night on the evening news. Exercising 60 minutes a day and following the food pyramid is not grabbing headlines like six-minute abs or the latest must-have supplement; it is boring. I often ask clients if they would rather be bored and wealthy, or excited and broke. It is human nature to seek out excitement, providing a constant difficulty for many to wrestle with when reviewing their plans.

Setting emotion aside, liquidity and tax concerns already addressed, *what* should you invest in? Smaller sums of money (perhaps $50,000 and under) are best diversified through the use of funds. Building a portfolio without concentration risk (the risk of large losses based on a single asset or sector) with less than $50,000 can be difficult. For people who really want to invest in a favorite stock or company, I might recommend opening a separate, smaller "play account" that is not considered part of the overall financial plan. Unintentional concentration risk is commonly found within Employee Stock Ownership Plans (ESOP), or retirement plans with company stock incentives, which cause the employee to have an overweighted position in one company—their employer.

So, how to begin?

Investment Funds

Mutual funds have long been considered the easiest way to diversify a portfolio without a huge financial commitment. The first open-end mutual fund was established in 1924 with the Massachusetts Investors Trust, and is still in existence at the time of this writing, and managed by MFS Investments Management.[24] A mutual fund pools investors' money to buy stocks, bonds, and other investments, typically run by investment managers who decide what to buy. The concept is like buying a small slice of a big, diversified pie, getting exposure to all the investments the fund owns.

As of 2024, there are over 7,000 mutual funds in the U.S. holding $29 trillion of assets.[25] Most company retirement plans offer a lineup of mutual funds for participants to choose from. These funds can reduce the concentration risk found in holding a single stock or bond, but they can still possess sector risk. Of the 7,000 mutual funds mentioned, many focus on a particular sector, such as information technology, emerging markets, or precious metals.

In 1993, an alternative to mutual funds was created in the U.S.'s first Exchange-Traded Fund (ETF), S&P 500 SPDR from State Street Global Investors.[26] ETFs are usually passively managed and track a market index

[24] Farina, Richard H.; Freeman, John P.; Webster, James (1969). "The Mutual Fund Industry: A Legal Survey." *Notre Dame Law Review*. 44: 732–983.

[25] https://www.ici.org/research/stats/trends_11_24#:~:text=Trends%20in%20Mutual%20Fund%20Investing%20November%202024,official%20survey%20of%20the%20mutual%20fund%20industry.

[26] https://www.investopedia.com/articles/exchangetradedfunds/12/brief-history-exchange-traded-funds.asp#citation-9

or sector sub-index, whereas mutual funds are typically actively managed, although not always. For this reason, ETFs often have a lower fee structure than mutual funds. ETFs can be bought and sold throughout the trading day just like stocks, whereas mutual funds are purchased at the end of each trading day. As of 2024, there were approximately 3,500 ETFs listed in the U.S. with $9 trillion of assets.[27]

ETFs gained wide consumer adoption through the strategy of "indexing." There have been many studies that show that actively managed portfolios, with a management fee, have underperformed their bench mark index. That is not to say all, as some actively managed mutual funds have outperformed their benchmarks. Indexing allows investors to bypass active management, choosing to *participate* in the market rather than *beat* the market, with little to no fee.

Index funds can be either mutual funds or ETFs. As of this writing, the largest Exchange-Traded Fund in the world is the original SPDR S&P 500 ETF (SPY) with over $600 billion in net assets. The largest mutual fund at the time is the Vanguard Total Stock Market Index Admiral (VTSAX) with nearly $1.8 trillion of net assets. Note that the largest funds on both sides are index funds.[28]

As an investor mulls over mutual funds and ETFs, or perhaps individual stocks and bonds, the first consideration is risk/reward. One of the traditional methods of portfolio creation is to identify one's risk tolerance on a scale of 1–10, 1 being conservative and 10 being aggressive, and then allocate the conservative portion to fixed income (bonds) and the aggressive portion to equities (stocks). For example, someone who scores a "6" risk rating would have a portfolio of 60 percent equities and

[27] https://www.jpmorgan.com/insights/global-research/investing/etf-guide#:~:text=U.S.%20ETF%20market&text=As%20of%20the%20end%20of%20May%202024%2C%20there%20were%20around,of%20the%20global%20ETF%20AUM).

[28] Yahoo! Finance (01/09/2025)

40 percent fixed income. Another school of thought, one which ignores risk tolerance and focuses on risk capacity, is to take 100, subtract your age, and put that amount in equities (i.e. 100 – 30 years old = 70 percent equities and 30 percent fixed income).

It is critical that conservative investors who consider fixed income recognize that there may still be risk involved. Unless they are purchasing cash equivalents, CDs backed by FDIC-insured banks, or treasuries backed by the U.S. government, bonds and bond funds are still a form of risk-bearing investing. Bonds contain default risk and interest rate risk. Default risk is the risk of the bond issuer becoming insolvent and unable to repay the bondholder. For this reason, issuers of publicly traded bonds are graded by the major credit rating agencies, ranging from investment-grade (high probability of repayment) to high-yield or "junk bonds" (lower probability of repayment).

Interest rate risk affects the valuation of bonds, as when interest rates go up, bond values go down. For example, bonds being issued at 5 percent today are more valuable to investors than ones issued years ago at 2 percent. Conversely, when interest rates fall, bond values rise. This dichotomy is often nicknamed the "seesaw effect." The year 2022 was a great example of how fixed income may not appear so "fixed" as asset classes in both stocks and bonds fell. When the Federal Reserve rapidly raised interest rates to fight inflation, the Total Bond Index (which tracks U.S. investment-grade bonds) lost over 13 percent for its worst year ever. Conservative investors positioned in bonds were blindsided by interest rate risk as their portfolios fell, often without any exposure to the stock market.[29]

[29] All investments contain risk and may lose value. **Past performance is not a guarantee of future results. Indices are unmanaged and one cannot invest directly in an index.** Investing in the bond market is subject to certain risks including market, interest rate, issuer, credit and inflation risk. Equities may decline in value due to both real and perceived general market, economic and industry conditions.

DON'T FIGHT THE FED

The Federal Reserve's involvement brings about another investment tenet, "Don't fight the Fed." The Fed is responsible for monetary policy, which entails the U.S. money supply and interest rates. When the Fed lowers the federal funds interest rate (the interest rate that banks charge each other for overnight loans), it fosters expansive lending, greater liquidity, and usually a boost to the stock market. Conversely, when the Fed increases rates ("restrictive policy"), it can slow lending, reduce the money supply, and affect the stock market negatively. With the stock market being considered a measure of liquidity, Fed policy regarding interest rates presents a powerful influencing factor.

The Fed is tasked with a dual mandate: maintain a low unemployment rate (generally considered 4 percent) and stabilize inflation (target rate of 2 percent). The irony is that helping one can hurt the other. Under normal conditions, cutting interest rates can reduce unemployment through a larger money supply available to the economy and businesses hiring employees. However, these same boosts to money supply, employment, and as a byproduct, the stock market, can also boost inflation. Conversely, when the Fed cuts interest rates to attack inflation, it often hampers business, leading to layoffs and/or a slowdown in hiring, and increased unemployment.

Economists often debate whether the Fed is proactive or reactive. When the economy experiences a downturn or recession, many argue that the Fed is not proactive enough and is partially to blame, if not entirely. In reality, the Fed prides itself on being data-dependent, and since data represents what has already occurred, the Fed is technically always reactive. Rather than debating proactive versus reactive, the better judgment is how active the Fed should be.

This balancing act involving unemployment and inflation can have an enormous impact on investors. The saying popularized in 2022 of "good news is bad news, and bad news is good news" implies that low unemployment (a good thing) allows the Fed to confidently increase rates or maintain restrictive policy, which hampers the stock market. On the other hand, increased unemployment (a bad thing) encourages the Fed to cut rates or maintain loose economic policy, which can bolster the stock market. While financial pundits pay close attention to monthly unemployment and inflation readings, these data points and Fed reactions often have immediate short-term effects, whereas in the long run, good news is good news and bad news is bad news.

If you are still asking yourself, "How can good news be bad news (or at least short-term bad news) and vice versa?" Remember that the stock market is a leading economic indicator. The Efficient Market Hypothesis (EMH), made famous by economist Eugene Fama, states that asset prices reflect all available information and are fair. Following this line of thinking, as soon as a piece of information becomes public, say an uptick in inflation, investors are immediately aware of the situation, its expected impact on the economy and influence on the Fed's monetary policy, and buys and sells on particular asset classes are instantly transacted based on the predicted outcome of these factors. The mentality is not all that different from a slew of bettors placing a bet on the Super Bowl after learning one team's quarterback injured his throwing arm; it is an informed investment prediction.

This forward-thinking characteristic of the stock market is what creates "value" and "growth" stocks/sectors. A new investor would not be foolish to think that the stock market would value a company for what it's worth. A profitable company with a good balance sheet should go up, and another operating at a loss, burdened in debt, should go down, right? Kind of, but the fickle nature of the stock market is always present.

Growth stocks are generally considered to be companies with a high price-to-earnings (P/E) ratio. This is not the only metric to consider, but it is widely recognized among companies that seemingly trade at a higher share price compared to their earnings. Why does a company with lower earnings trade for a higher price? Simply put, investors think there's a bright future ahead. Growth stocks are most synonymous with the tech sector, companies known for reinvesting large portions of their profits in research and development (R&D) and taking on debt to pursue new ideas with the exciting hopes of disrupting the industry. Some growth companies grow far beyond investor expectations, think of Amazon or Apple in their early innings, while others never grow and eventually leave investors sorely disappointed.

Value stocks are the exact opposite; they appear to be trading at a discount with relatively low P/E ratios. Investors have to weigh whether the stock or sector is truly a discount being overlooked, or if it is priced correctly as its decline is on the horizon.

WHAT DID I DO?

First, I will tell you about the very beginning, and then I'll tell you about the real beginning.

The very beginning occurred during my junior year of college. Through my various campus jobs and summer work, I saved up what I thought was enough to consider myself an investor. I took $500 from my savings account and opened a brokerage account with Scottrade (eventually acquired by TD Ameritrade, which was then acquired by Charles Schwab). I played around with a stock screener and deliberated over what would be my first investment with great scrutiny, as I braced myself for the $7 transaction fee once I clicked "BUY," and knowing it would be there again when I clicked "SELL."

After doing my due diligence, I decided on ticker symbol SIX (Six Flags, Inc.). It was a company I was familiar with, its share price was low enough that I could buy a decent amount of shares with my $500, and all of the credit rating agencies gave it stellar reviews. It was considered a value stock with its low share price against relatively decent earnings and assets.

My experience underscores the timeless investment adage to "invest in what you know." The credit rating agencies assigned SIX very strong ratings based on a variety of financial measures. However, as I clicked BUY, I thought about the past couple of times I visited Six Flags Great Adventure in Jackson, NJ. There was trash everywhere, most of the rides were broken, the lines were long with disgruntled patrons, and it just wasn't the good time I remembered. Fast forward a couple of years, and Six Flags, Inc., the company so many "financial gurus" promoted, declared bankruptcy.[30] As a result, my shares were eliminated in a Chapter 11 reorganization, and my entire investment was wiped out. I abandoned what I knew about the company and paid the price. As bad as this financial loss hurt my poor college self, it was a good lesson learned at a relatively low cost in the scheme of life.

The real beginning started after I graduated from college and began my profession as a financial advisor. Per my own advice, the first year of my career was spent avoiding debt and building up my savings account. Plain, simple, and boring, but very necessary.

With one full year of work under my belt, I made two new financial decisions. I became eligible for my company's 401(k) plan and began contributing up to the employer match of 3 percent. I did not go above the match as pre-tax was the only contribution option at the time, and I did not want to create a compounding unknown future tax liability, and I was still focused on building liquidity as a 23-year-old. I set up my 401(k) allocation to be 100 percent equities, a mix of mostly large-cap domestic

[30] https://archive.nytimes.com/dealbook.nytimes.com/2009/06/13/six-flags-files-for-bankruptcy/#:~:text=By%20Michael%20J.,the%20Company%20for%20future%20growth.%E2%80%9D

funds and some small-cap and international exposure. I had met with a successful hedge fund manager who had a huge 401(k) and he said his father, who was even more successful, told him on his first day of work to invest in 100 percent equities. A 23-year-old me followed this advice on a leap of faith, but the more I have experienced, the more I agree with his recommendation. I have since increased to maxing out my 401(k) and mostly on a Roth basis.

I have never changed this very aggressive allocation as I am aware how long-term the account is and historically equities have outperformed bonds. I also opened a Whole Life policy with a $100 monthly premium. While technically this is not an investment, I locked in my insurability with the best health rating while I was young and healthy, and its cash value began accruing interest and dividends with its favorable tax treatment.

The next year, with my savings growing and 401(k) and Whole Life plan underway, I opened a Roth IRA, which I began making maximum annual contributions to. This is composed primarily of individual stocks. I consider it my ultra-aggressive "play account." While I do not day trade, this account is my most actively traded account, as I am not concerned with tax ramifications since it grows tax-free. I still continue the same funding and investing approach today with "Backdoor Roth IRA" contributions, a two-step process of making nondeductible contributions to a Traditional IRA, which are immediately converted into the Roth.

I then purchased my first home, a condo with a conventional 30-year fixed-rate mortgage and 20 percent down payment. I have since moved, but still own this as a rental property. Through my late 20s and early 30s, I began adding more condo rental properties. Real estate has always seemed to have a great appeal to investors. I was told by a very successful real estate investor early in my career that it is a patient way to get wealthy. The concept of a multi-benefit investment, including passive rental income, capital appreciation of the property, and a tenant funding your mortgage, is attractive. But, real estate can be far more capital-intensive, hands-on, with an array of extra costs, when compared to traditional investing.

Once comfortably settled into my budget with my new home, I added a second, larger Whole Life plan and opened a non-qualified taxable investment account (technical title of what most people just consider a brokerage account). Some people might be confused as to why I added a second life insurance policy as a young single guy with no kids. I viewed these, and still do, as a slow, steady way to accumulate wealth in addition to the life insurance benefits it will one day afford me. Their cash values grow at a guaranteed rate, tax-deferred, accessible tax-free, with a disability waiver of premium to continue funding them should I become sick or hurt, providing a safe foundation to my fixed income portion of my balance sheet.

I initially opened my brokerage account with what are referred to in the industry as TAMPs (Third Party Asset Managers). These are portfolios that advisors utilize for their clients, which are actively managed by outside firms. Early in my career, these were strongly encouraged. The advisor, Me, would be the macro advisor, and the TAMP would be the micro advisor. Over time, I found this to be cumbersome, layered with additional fees, and most TAMPs underperformed their benchmark. After a couple of years, I liquidated these accounts and consolidated them into my own personally managed account. I periodically sweep excess cash into this "slush fund" every few months.

My brokerage account allocation is one that some would consider controversial. A portion of it is safely invested in short-term treasuries that I view as working capital for potential real estate opportunities or other life events. The majority of it, though, is invested in the stock market—a changing diversified portfolio usually including a few individual stocks, a rare minerals ETF, and technology, healthcare, large cap value, and S&P 500 funds (summary as of 2025, these allocations are subject to change but follow an overall moderate risk stance with historically an overweight to tech). The controversial part is the way in which I am exposed to the S&P 500, my core holding.

For several years, I have owned ticker symbol SSO (Proshares Ultra S&P 500), a leveraged ETF that seeks daily investment results, before fees and expenses, that correspond to two times (2x) the daily performance of the S&P 500.[31] My theory is simple: if indexing works over the long term, particularly through the S&P 500, then why not do it twice as well?

I must disclose that as an advisor, my broker/dealer does not allow me to invest in any leveraged products for my clients. This is for good reason. Doubling a rising market is fantastic, but doubling a falling market can be terrifying for most investors. I would never consider allocating or maintaining any funds in this particular holding that I do not absolutely consider to be long-term money. I do not seek to time the market, as alluded to earlier in this chapter, but utilizing this fund is the closest I come to such an approach. I have made larger-than-ordinary contributions to the holding during market pullbacks exceeding 10 percent.

This is my investment approach in summary: six months' expenses in cash, Whole Life cash values as a safe haven, moderate brokerage account, and ultra-aggressive retirement plans mostly funded on a Roth basis. My annual cash flow allocation (not including sporadic real estate investing) is currently as follows: 22% to retirement plans, 10% to Whole Life, and 68% to taxable brokerage account. It is not for everyone, and it does not work best all the time, but I am looking for it to work *over* time. I aim to hold the same exact investments as my clients, aside from my S&P 500 allocation being leveraged whereas theirs is not. The only type of holding that many of my clients possess which I do not are a variety of annuities geared towards retirement which simply are not suitable for my age category.

My greatest tests, like most people, have come during market downturns. 2018 wasn't enough to worry me, but the rapid market collapse during the COVID-19 pandemic in the spring of 2020 and the market correction during the inflation battle of 2022 were a gut check for me as both an investor and a fiduciary. I did not sell any positions during both downturns in my own portfolio or that of my clients, and continued systematic investments on both fronts. Was I worried? Of course. I read

[31] https://www.proshares.com/our-etfs/leveraged-and-inverse/sso

all the historical data, studied charts, spoke with experienced asset managers, but still, until you see the account balances go back up, you truly do not know that they will go up. Fortunately, faith in the process saw me and my clients through to brighter days.

FREQUENTLY ASKED QUESTIONS

When should I start investing?

Answer: The sooner the better, but *not* before Steps 1–3 have been fully addressed. For my clients, the minimum to open a passively-managed investment account is $1,000, and the minimum automatic investment I allow is $100 monthly, whereas my actively managed portfolio currently has a $50,000 minimum. There are investment platforms that can start with less, but I find these values to be worthwhile.

Is there a time when it is too late to start investing?

Answer: No. As long as an investor has a three-plus year horizon for their money, whether it is for their own benefit or maybe to leave behind as a legacy, then there may be opportunities to invest. I often caution retired investors from automatically thinking all their assets must be conservative simply because of their age; if an 80-year-old wealthy investor has set aside funds for legacy planning, then their real horizon may be based more on their children's and grandchildren's horizon than their own.

Should I use a financial advisor, a robo-advisor, or self-manage my portfolio?

Answer: This largely depends on how involved you want to be in the ongoing management of your investments and coordination with overall financial plans. An investor who is fully satisfied dollar-cost-averaging into a large-cap index fund with a long horizon may be able to thrive on their own. However, as their financial plans evolve and natural emotional tendencies begin to sway their decisions, having an experienced Certified Financial Planner™ as a co-pilot can help.

How often should I rebalance my portfolio?

Answer: There is no perfect answer, but for diversified portfolios, I recommend every six months. Rebalancing in shorter intervals can interrupt rallies in the market, and longer intervals can risk the portfolio getting too far unbalanced. For ultra-aggressive investors who are in 100 percent equities, they may not want to rebalance and just keep their foot on the pedal, hoping growing companies keep growing. Conversely, very conservative investors may continue in 100 percent fixed income for fear of the stock market, no matter how beaten down it may be.

Should I use annuities?

Answer: *Annuities* are insurance products that can come in many forms and are commonly used for retirement planning. It is a large segment of wealth planning as according to LIMRA, there was over $432 billion of new annuity sales in 2024.[32] Depending on the product, it can provide guaranteed income in retirement similar to social security benefits or a defined benefit pension, tax-deferred growth, and/or downside protection against stock market risk. Most annuities have a surrender schedule that can restrict access to the funds for a period of time. Depending on how they are designed, the fee structure can vary, supporting the thought that certain benefits are not "too good to be true, just too good to be free." Like any other investment, whether it is good or bad depends largely on your financial goals. Here is a summary of the various annuity types:

[32] "2024 Retail Annuity Sales Power to a Record $432.4 Billion." LIMRA (01/28/2025).

- **Fixed Annuity**. This offers a guaranteed rate of return on your principal, similar to a bank Certificate of Deposit (CD) for a set number of years.
- **Variable Annuity**. This offers upside potential based on the performance of underlying mutual funds selected inside the annuity. For an additional fee, riders can be purchased that can offer guaranteed Single or Joint lifetime income and/or enhanced death benefits.
- **Fixed Indexed Annuity**. This can offer upside potential based on the performance of an underlying index up to a cap, but with a minimum interest rate or floor.
- **Registered Index-Linked Annuity**. This combines features of fixed and variable annuities, typically offering potential for market growth based on an index (like the S&P 500) up to a cap, but with a "buffer" that can absorb a percentage of losses in down years.

Remember, hard work is good, but hard-working money is great. One should not replace the other, as a hard worker without investments might work themselves into the ground, and an investor without hard work is bound to be let down by the reality of needing a paycheck to fund their investments. I have seen smart investing provide a huge boost to people's financial situation, but I have seen few to none who made their fortunes *solely* by investing.

Investing should be fun. But in order to best behave with your investments, rather than begging your investments to behave with you, you must first know your own financial behavior and follow a process, not a product.

CONCLUSION

"Everything should be made as simple as possible,
but not simpler."
—Albert Einstein

These are four simple steps that I have followed myself as well as applied when advising clients—ranging from those just starting out to those worth fortunes. This four-step process has been proven to work under the broadest number of circumstances possible and has been time-tested with thousands of man hours in front of clients from nearly every background. I have learned along the way that a financial plan does not have to be exciting in and of itself; rather, satisfactory results are what should be exciting.

Kudos if you have completed this book cover-to-cover. There were likely parts of the journey that were of great interest, and others you thought had nothing to do with you. But whether you realize it or not, each of these steps helps to wash over your existing psychology towards money, leaving you more prepared for what lies ahead. You are a different person today than you were five years ago; you will be a different person in five years than you are today. These steps will carry different meaning to you through the phases of life, so feel free to revisit each section for a deeper understanding as needed.

Here is a quick summary of things to remember:

Know Thyself

Are you conservative or aggressive? Do you love winning or hate losing? As life goes on and you go through major events like marriage, the birth of a child, job changes, loss, economic rallies and collapses, always be ready to ask yourself: Who am I?

Am I Protected?

Even if it is just once a year, set up a routine time to ask yourself this question. New Year's works well, or your birthday, or when the kids go back to school. No matter when you get around to it, think carefully about all the what-ifs of life. Be the devil's advocate and mentally stress test your plans. What would happen if you lost your job? Got sick? Were sued? The markets tanked?

Stay Liquid

Check your budget. Review your credit card bills over the past few months and see what the spending trend looks like. Do you have six times this available in savings? Are there any big projects for the year that you know carry an extra price tag?

Check Your Debts

Make sure your credit cards are paid off in full every month, without exception. If there are some high interest debts lingering, explore the options discussed in Step 3 for potential solutions and trading bad debts for good debts.

Is My Money Working as Hard as I Am?

At the end of every year, look at your gross income, calculate 20 percent of it, and see if you saved that much over the year. If not, consider increasing your automatic investment plans, even if just by another percentage point. Small adjustments matter—if you were to cruise around the world and adjust your rudder by a degree, you might end up on a different continent. It's the same with financial planning: a percentage here or there over 40 or 50 years can have an enormous difference. Your portfolio will look different based on your risk tolerance and risk capacity, but no matter what allocation you set, remember to rebalance it accordingly every six months or so.

Simple is not always easy, but it is achievable and repeatable. I hope this roadmap can help to free you of financial worry, put you on the right track, and allow you to pursue the important things in life: wealth… state of well-being.

DISCLAIMER

This material is intended for general use. By providing this content The Guardian Life Insurance Company of America, Park Avenue Securities LLC, affiliates and/or subsidiaries, and your financial representative are not undertaking to provide advice or make a recommendation for a specific individual or situation, or to otherwise act in a fiduciary capacity. Guardian, its subsidiaries, agents and employees do not provide tax, legal, or accounting advice. Consult your tax, legal, or accounting professional regarding your individual situation.

This material contains the current opinions of Bryan Kuderna but not necessarily those of Guardian or its subsidiaries and such opinions are subject to change without notice.

This material has not been endorsed by Guardian, its subsidiaries, agents, or employees. No representation or warranty, either express or implied, is provided in relation to the accuracy, completeness, or reliability of the information contained herein. In addition, the content does not necessarily represent the opinions of Guardian, its subsidiaries, agents, or employees.

Data and rates used were indicative of market conditions as of the date shown. Opinions, estimates, forecasts and statements of financial market trends are based on current market conditions and are subject to change without notice. References to specific securities, asset classes and financial markets are for illustrative purposes only and do not constitute a solicitation, offer, or recommendation to purchase or sell a security. Past performance is not a guarantee of future results.

ABOUT THE AUTHOR

Bryan Kuderna is a Certified Financial Planner® and the founder of Kuderna Financial Team. Named one of New Jersey's Top 10 Financial Professionals of 2021 by NJBiz, he also hosts a popular finance and business podcast, The Kuderna Podcast. He is a regular contributor to Fox Business, CNBC, Yahoo Finance, AARP, and other media. His first book, *Millennial Millionaire*, launched Kuderna as a national speaker at colleges, hospitals, corporations, and financial institutions and paved the way for his book, *What Should I Do With My Money?*. Kuderna has a Master of Science in Financial Services from The American College and a Bachelor of Science in Finance and Economics from The College of New Jersey. Bryan lives in New Jersey with his wife and three children.